Pocket

BARCELONA

TOP SIGHTS • LOCAL LIFE • MADE EASY

D1009292

Regis St Louis

In This Book

QuickStart Guide

Your keys to understanding the city – we help you decide what to do and how to do it

Need to Know
Tips for a smooth trip

Neighbourhoods
What's where

Explore Barcelona

The best things to see and do, neighbourhood by neighbourhood

Top Sights
Make the most of your visit

Local Life
The insider's city

The Best of Barcelona

The city's highlights in handy lists to help you plan

Best Walks
See the city on foot

Barcelona's Best...
The best experiences

Survival Guide

Tips and tricks for a seamless, hassle-free city experience

Getting Around
Travel like a local

Essential Information
Including where to stay

Our selection of the city's best places to eat, drink and experience:

◉ **Sights**

✖ **Eating**

◯ **Drinking**

✪ **Entertainment**

🔓 **Shopping**

These symbols give you the vital information for each listing:

☏ Telephone Numbers		👪 Family-Friendly
⊙ Opening Hours		🚌 Bus
P Parking		⛴ Ferry
@ Internet Access		M Metro
🛜 Wi-Fi Access		🚋 Tram
✔ Vegetarian Selection		🚈 Train

Find each listing quickly on maps for each neighbourhood:

Bar Hemingway

16 ◯ Map p233, B2

Legend has it that Hemi self, wielding a machine rate this timber-pan ered bar during showpiece is a en by Papa an town. Dress s.com; Hôtel Rit ⊙6.30pm-2a

Lonely Planet's Barcelona

Lonely Planet Pocket Guides are designed to get you straight to the heart of the city.

Inside you'll find all the must-see sights, plus tips to make your visit to each one really memorable. We've split the city into easy-to-navigate neighbourhoods and provided clear maps so you'll find your way around with ease. Our expert authors have searched out the best of the city: walks, food, nightlife and shopping, to name a few. Because you want to explore, our 'Local Life' pages will take you to some of the most exciting areas to experience the real Barcelona.

And of course you'll find all the practical tips you need for a smooth trip: itineraries for short visits, how to get around, and how much to tip the guy who serves you a drink at the end of a long day's exploration.

It's your guarantee of a really great experience.

Our Promise

You can trust our travel information because Lonely Planet authors visit the places we write about, each and every edition. We never accept freebies for positive coverage, so you can rely on us to tell it like it is.

QuickStart Guide 7

Barcelona Top Sights............ **8**

Barcelona Local Life **12**

Barcelona Day Planner **14**

Need to Know...................... **16**

Barcelona
Neighbourhoods **18**

Explore Barcelona 21

22 La Rambla & Barri Gòtic

42 El Raval

54 La Ribera & Parc de la Ciutadella

74 Barceloneta & the Beaches

86 Passeig de Gràcia & L'Eixample

114 Montjuïc, Poble Sec & Sant Antoni

132 Camp Nou, Pedralbes & Sarrià

Worth a Trip:

La Sagrada Família **106**

Village Life in Gràcia **110**

Park Güell............................ **112**

The Best of Barcelona 141

Barcelona's Best Walks

The Old City in a Day............142
Modernista Barcelona............144
Food-Lovers' Barcelona............146

Barcelona's Best ...

Restaurants............148
Shopping............150
Tapas............152
Architecture............154
Art & Design............156
Parks & Beaches............158
Sports & Activities............160
Views............161
Museums............162
For Kids............164
Tours............166
For Free............167
Bars............168
Cafes............170
Clubs............172
Gay & Lesbian............173
Live Music & the Arts............174

Survival Guide 175

Before You Go............176
Arriving in Barcelona............178
Getting Around............179
Essential Information............180
Language............184

QuickStart Guide

Barcelona Top Sights..8

Barcelona Local Life..12

Barcelona Day Planner 14

Need to Know..16

Barcelona Neighbourhoods 18

Welcome to Barcelona

Barcelona could just be the coolest city on earth. Style conscious and always in fashion, this is a place where the avant-garde and the traditional collide daily with spectacular results. It's where Gaudí meets Gothic, where food is life in all its delicious complexity, and where the arts (including the art of having a good time) always take centre stage.

Spiral staircase, La Sagrada Família (p106)
CHRIS MELLOR/GETTY IMAGES ©

Barcelona
Top Sights

La Sagrada Família (p106)

A temple as much to originality in architecture as to God, the recently conse-crated La Sagrada Família is Gaudí's Modernista masterpiece and an extraordi-nary work in progress.

INIGO CIA/GETTY IMAGES ©

Park Güell (p112)

The playfulness of Gaudí's imagination takes flight in this park, which seems to spring from a child's fantasy of seriously weird structures and larger-than-life animal forms.

La Catedral (p28)

Barcelona's cathedral spans the centuries like a sombre and silent witness to the city's history. It's a towering edifice of singular and monumental beauty with a refined cloister inhabited by geese.

La Rambla (p24)

Few pedestrian thoroughfares can rival La Rambla as it cuts a swathe through old Barcelona and down to the shores of the Mediterranean. It's a canvas, a catwalk and a stage all in one.

Basílica de Santa Maria del Mar (p60)

This soaring Gothic church is a study in grace, harmony, symmetry and simplicity, and is a prime candidate for the title of our favourite traditional house of worship in the city.

Casa Batlló (p90)

Even Gaudí outdid himself with this fanciful apartment block: an astonishing confection of rippling balconies, coloured tiles, optical illusions and twisted chimney pots on Barcelona's grandest boulevard.

Museu Picasso (p56)

Pablo Picasso's enduring gift to the city he loved is this superb collection of the artist's early works – an intriguing study of Picasso's search for a style all his own.

Mercat de la Boqueria (p44)

One of Europe's great produce markets, this is also the centrepiece of Barcelona's culinary culture. You'll find buzzing tapas bars and uniquely Catalan produce all under one roof.

Museu Nacional d'Art de Catalunya (p116)

Home to Barcelona's finest art collection, this museum has Romanesque treasure from the Catalan Pyrenees, Venetian Renaissance masters and Catalan art.

La Pedrera (p88)

The fourth of Gaudí's unmissable Modernista gifts to the city, this apartment block is extraordinary both outside and within, a hallucinatory creation that only gets better the higher you climb.

Fundació Joan Miró (p120)

There is no finer or more comprehensive collection of Joan Miró's artistic endeavours than this museum. Miró is one of Barcelona's favourite sons and was a towering figure of 20th-century Catalan art.

Camp Nou & the Museu del FC Barcelona (p134)

In a city of temples and sacred turf, few rival the home of FC Barcelona for the passion it arouses. It's one of the greatest sporting stadiums on earth and a place of pilgrimage.

Barcelona Local Life

Insider tips to help you find the real city

If you're eager to experience Barcelona rather than merely tick off its signature attractions, we'll show you how the locals experience their city – traditional tapas bars and flea markets, Catalan traditional dances and local drinking holes that haven't changed in decades.

A Barri Gòtic Sunday (p30)

▶ Local markets
▶ Traditional dance

In the most heavily touristed part of the city, locals reclaim their *barrio* (neighbourhood) on Sundays. Join them at a mass in the 14th-century church where Gaudí was once arrested, then enjoy back-to-basics markets, visit icons of Catalan power and discover timeless local eating haunts.

Revelling in El Raval (p46)

▶ Bastions of tradition
▶ Gritty streets

El Raval is Barcelona's most diverse neighbourhood, at once stylish and slightly louche in the manner of port cities down through the centuries. From the refined to the bohemian, it's a journey through cultures and countercultures with detours to ageless Catalan classics en route.

Tapas & Bar-Hopping in El Born (p62)

▶ Tapas bars
▶ Nightlife

So much of life in Barcelona as the locals experience it revolves around food, and El Born, a tight tangle of medieval streets near La Ribera's southern edge, is one of the best (and prettiest) places in town to go out for tapas and drinks.

Sea & Seafood (p76)

▶ Fish restaurants
▶ Beaches

A bulwark of busy bars and fish restaurants where old-style cooking prevails, the former fisherfolk district of Barceloneta has held fast to its traditions. But the shiny new Barcelona has grabbed hold of the surrounding beaches and marinas. These are two very different worlds in one city.

Shop in the Quadrat d'Or (p92)

▶ Designer boutiques
▶ Gourmet shops

One of Europe's grand shopping boulevards,

Barri Gòtic (p22)

the Passeig de Gràcia is stage to the city's top fashion boutiques. But L'Eixample's genius is to throw up a whole culture of shopping, with the greatest affections reserved for local names in design, furniture and high-quality foodstuffs.

Village Life in Gràcia (p110)

▶ Old-style plazas
▶ Markets & bars

On the cusp of downtown Barcelona yet somehow separate, Gràcia is a lovely mix of old and new, with markets, plazas, bars and restaurants that date back

decades alongside ultra-hip designer boutiques. The area is diverse and offbeat – just how the locals like it.

Nightlife in Sant Antoni & Poble Sec (p122)

▶ Terrace bars
▶ Tapas

Just below the looming mountain of Montjuïc, the pedestrian lanes of Poble Sec are dotted with tapas joints and bohemian drinking dens. The action continues across wide Av del Paral·lel, in Sant Antoni, with outdoor cafes and creative tapas bars.

Other great places to experience the city like a local:

Barri Gòtic cafes (p40)

Antic Hospital de la Santa Creu (p52)

Beach bars (p85)

Parc de la Ciutadella (p66)

Speakeasy (p99)

Filmoteca de Catalunya (p51)

El Passadís del Pep (p69)

Carrer de Blai (p130)

Sarrià (p138)

Aire de Barcelona (p70)

Barcelona
Day Planner

Day One

☀ Begin with Barcelona's standout sight, the otherworldly **La Sagrada Família** (p107), getting there early to avoid the queues. After a couple of hours (or more) acquiring a taste for Gaudí's flights of architectural fancy, head over to **La Pedrera** (p88) and **Casa Batlló** (p90). Browse for a while in **Vinçon** (p92) or shop for shoes in **Camper** (p104), then have a tapas lunch at **Tapas 24** (p144).

☀ After lunch, stroll the length of **La Rambla** (p24), then dive into the narrow lanes of Barcelona's oldest quarter, the Barri Gòtic. Begin in **Plaça Reial** (p34), move on to the **Església de Santa Maria del Pi** (p34), then finish up at **La Catedral** (p28), but otherwise simply wander to get lost.

☾ As evening approaches, sample the best in Catalan tapas at **El Xampanyet** (p63), follow it up with some creative twists at **Bar del Pla** (p63), then move on to the enduringly popular **Cal Pep** (p69). Anywhere along **Passeig del Born** (p62) is great for night-time revelry, but our favourite perch is **La Vinya del Senyor** (p71).

Day Two

☀ Get an early start at the **Mercat de la Boqueria** (p44), wandering amid the market stalls and perhaps stopping for breakfast and a chat with Juanito at **Bar Pinotxo** (p51). It's always worth checking out the exhibitions at the **Museu d'Art Contemporani de Barcelona** (p49) and the **Centre de Cultura Contemporània de Barcelona** (p50). Stop off for a hot chocolate at **Granja M Viader** (p47) and lunch at **Suculent** (p51).

☀ **Palau Güell** (p49) is a wonderful way to start the afternoon. After an hour there, head across the old city to the sublime **Basílica de Santa Maria del Mar** (p60) for an hour of quiet contemplation, followed by a couple of hours at the **Museu Picasso** (p56), one of Barcelona's most rewarding museums.

☾ Candle-lit **La Vinateria del Call** (p36) is a great old-city choice for a sit-down Catalan meal, followed by tea in atmospheric **Salterio** (p40). Otherwise, make an early tapas stop at **Belmonte** (p36) and head for an uplifting live performance at the **Gran Teatre del Liceu** (p40). Afterwards take a nightcap in lively **Ocaña** (p38) on Plaça Reial.

Short on time?
We've arranged Barcelona's must-sees into these day-by-day itineraries to make sure you see the very best of the city in the time you have available.

Day Three

After an early morning stroll down La Rambla, drop off its southern end to **La Rambla del Mar** (p80), as a precursor to a morning by the sea. Pause for a lesson in Catalan history at the **Museu d'Història de Catalunya** (p80), then dive into the old fishing district of **La Barceloneta**, emerging on the other side for a stroll along the beach. For lunch, have a seafood feast with waterfront views at **Barraca** (p82).

For some of the best views in Barcelona, take the **Transbordador Aeri** (p80) cable car across to Montjuïc. The area's museums, vantage points and gardens are all worth exploring, but a couple of hours each at the marvellous **Fundació Joan Miró** (p120) and **Museu Nacional d'Art de Catalunya** (p116) will keep you busy all afternoon.

At the foot of the Montjuïc hill, **Quimet i Quimet** (p130) is one of our favourite tapas bars in town. Afterwards, have a drink at bordello-esque **Rouge Lab 2.1** (p123), then stroll over to **Bar Calders** (p123) in Sant Antoni.

Day Four

Use the morning to immerse yourself in two of Barcelona's most iconic (if very different) sights: the weird and utterly wonderful playground-like **Park Güell** (p112), where Gaudí's fertile imagination ran riot, and a stadium tour at the home of FC Barcelona, **Camp Nou** (p134). Both are worth a couple of hours. Afterwards head up to Sarrià for a meal at **Vivanda** (p138) and a wander through the village-like lanes.

Head back to the old city for a tour of the **Palau de la Música Catalana** (p66) and spend some time soaking up the neighbourhood-market feel of the **Mercat de Santa Caterina** (p66). Hop on the metro up to L'Eixample's **Passeig de Gràcia** for some of Europe's best shopping (p104). Spend some much-needed downtime over a velvety red wine at **Monvínic** (p93).

A last night in Barcelona deserves something special: a splurge at the Michelin-starred **Cinc Sentits** (p98) or the Gaudí-decorated **Casa Calvet** (p101). After a refined cocktail or two at **Dry Martini** (p103), take one last stroll down **La Rambla** (p24) to bid farewell to the city.

Need to Know

For more information, see Survival Guide (p175)

Currency
Euro (€)

Language
Spanish (Castellano) and Catalan

Visas
Generally not required for stays of up to 90 days (not at all for members of EU or Schengen countries). Some nationalities need a Schengen visa.

Money
ATMs widely available. Credit cards accepted in most hotels, restaurants and shops.

Mobile Phones
Local SIM cards can be used in British/European and Australian phones. US and other travellers' phones need to be set to roaming.

Time
Western European (GMT/UTC plus one hour, or plus two hours during daylight savings).

Plugs & Adaptors
Plugs have two round pins; the standard electrical current is 230V.

Tipping
Small change (€1 per person in restaurants) and rounding up (in taxis) is usually sufficient.

① Before You Go

Your Daily Budget

Budget less than €100
▶ Dorm bed €15–20; *hostal* double €50–70
▶ Cheaper three-course lunch *menú del día*
▶ Plan sightseeing for free admission times

Midrange €100–200
▶ Midrange hotel double €75–150
▶ Lunch in decent restaurant €40 for two
▶ Use discount cards to keep costs down

Top End more than €200
▶ Double room in top-end hotel from €150
▶ Evening fine dining from €50 per person

Useful Websites

▶ **Barcelona Turisme** (www.barcelonaturisme.com) The city's official tourism website.

▶ **Miniguide** (miniguide.es) Restaurants and bars, upcoming events and theatre reviews.

▶ **Barcelona Metropolitan** (www.barcelona-metropolitan.com) New restaurant openings, nightlife reviews and city profiles.

▶ **Lonely Planet** (www.lonelyplanet.com/barcelona) Destination information, hotel bookings, traveller forums and more.

Advance Planning

▶ **Three months before** Book your hotel early to increase choice and reduce price; weekends can book out months in advance.

▶ **One month before** Book a table at Tickets tapas bar (www.ticketsbar.es) or Cinc Sentits restaurant (www.cincsentits.com).

▶ **One week before** Book online entry to La Sagrada Família and Museu Picasso to avoid queues on arrival.

② Arriving in Barcelona

Most visitors arrive at Aeroport del Prat (www.barcelona-airport.com), 12km southwest of the city. Some carriers land at Aeroport de Girona–Costa Brava (www.girona-airport.net), 90km north of Barcelona. The main train station is Estació de Sants, 2.5km west of La Rambla.

✈ From Aeroport del Prat

Destination	Best Transport
Barri Gòtic	A1 Aerobús; Metro (line 3)
El Raval	A1 Aerobús; Metro (line 3)
La Ribera	A1 Aerobús; Metro (lines 1, 4)
La Barceloneta	A1 Aerobús; Metro (lines 1, 4)
L'Eixample	R2 Nord Train

✈ From Aeroport de Girona–Costa Brava

Destination	Best Transport
Barri Gòtic	Barcelona Bus; Metro (lines 1, 3)
El Raval	Barcelona Bus; Metro (lines 1, 3)
La Ribera	Barcelona Bus
La Barceloneta	Barcelona Bus; Metro (lines 1, 4)
L'Eixample	Barcelona Bus; Metro (lines 1, 3)

✈ At the Airports

Aeroport del Prat Terminal 1 and 2 arrivals halls have ATMs and tourist information.

Aeroport de Girona–Costa Brava The baggage-claim and arrivals halls have ATMs.

③ Getting Around

Barcelona has an efficient and comprehensive public transport system. Apart from getting into town from the airport, the Metro (www.tmb.net) is the best way for getting around town. For some outlying areas, the Metro is supplemented by the FGC (www.fgc.net) suburban rail network. Conveniently, both operate under the same ticketing system (as do city buses); it works out cheaper to purchase the 10-trip T-10 ticket (€10.30) rather than buying individual tickets.

Ⓜ Metro

Eight colour-coded Metro lines crisscross central Barcelona. Metro stations circle the old city (the Barri Gòtic, El Raval and La Ribera), and the Metro leaves you on the perimeter of La Barceloneta. There are also stations all across L'Eixample.

🚇 FGC

The suburban rail network is particularly useful for Pedralbes, Sarrià and Gràcia. Stations in the town centre include Passeig de Gràcia and Plaça de Catalunya.

🚡 Funicular

A funicular railway (part of the Metro) connects Paral·lel Metro station to the stations up the hill in Montjuïc; these additional stations are part of the Telefèric de Montjuïc, require separate tickets, and carry you to the summit. The Transbordador Aeri cable car connects La Barceloneta with Montjuïc.

🚕 Taxi

Taxis can be hailed on the street or you can call for one. Taking a cab across town can be convenient outside peak traffic times.

🚲 Bicycle

Barcelona has over 180km of bike lanes. The city has numerous bike-hire outlets, but note that the red 'Bicing' bikes are for local residents only.

Barcelona
Neighbourhoods

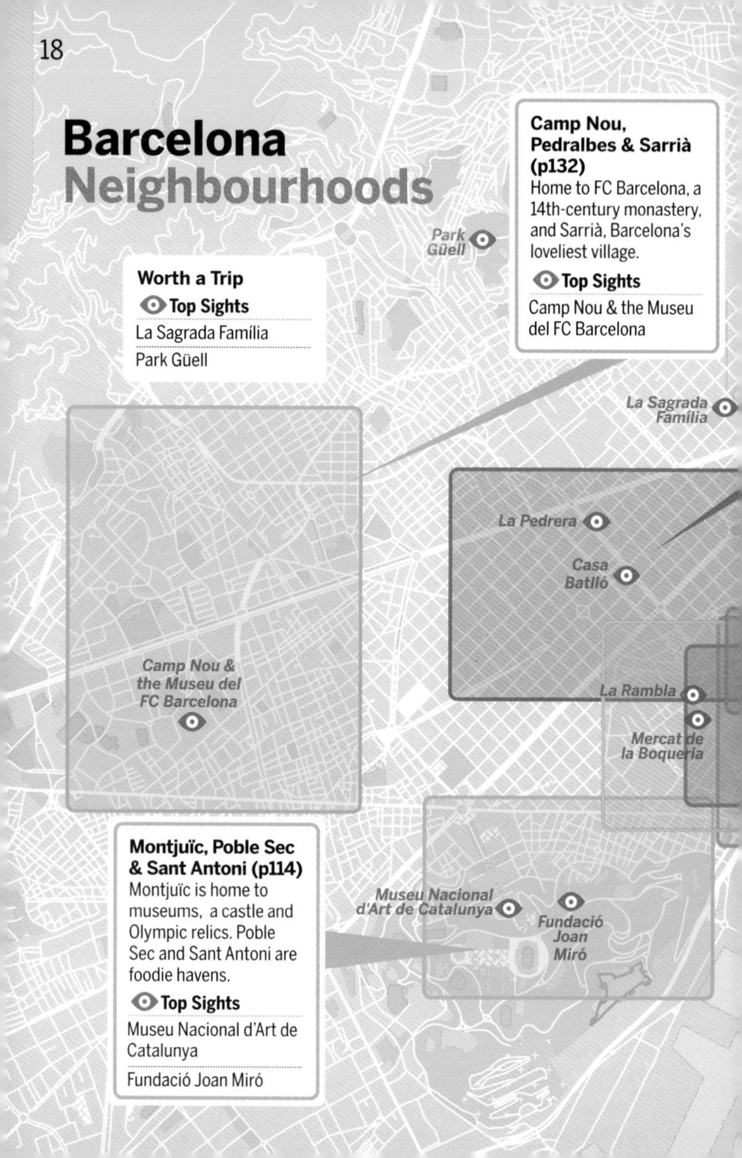

Camp Nou, Pedralbes & Sarrià (p132)

Home to FC Barcelona, a 14th-century monastery, and Sarrià, Barcelona's loveliest village.

⊙ Top Sights

Camp Nou & the Museu del FC Barcelona

⊙ Park Güell

Worth a Trip

⊙ Top Sights

La Sagrada Família

Park Güell

⊙ La Sagrada Família

Camp Nou & the Museu del FC Barcelona

⊙ La Pedrera

⊙ Casa Batlló

⊙ La Rambla

⊙ Mercat de la Boqueria

Montjuïc, Poble Sec & Sant Antoni (p114)

Montjuïc is home to museums, a castle and Olympic relics. Poble Sec and Sant Antoni are foodie havens.

⊙ Top Sights

Museu Nacional d'Art de Catalunya

Fundació Joan Miró

⊙ Museu Nacional d'Art de Catalunya

⊙ Fundació Joan Miró

Passeig de Gràcia & L'Eixample (p86)
Explore Modernista treasures, outstanding bars and restaurants, and a shopper's paradise to rival Paris.

⊙ Top Sights

La Pedrera

Casa Batlló

La Ribera & Parc de la Ciutadella (p54)
La Ribera has a wonderful market, splendid architecture, plus El Born district – Barcelona's byword for cool.

⊙ Top Sights

Museu Picasso

Basílica de Santa Maria del Mar

Barceloneta & the Beaches (p74)
Barcelona as it once was with an age-old culture of fishing, and an altogether shinier new beach culture.

Museu Picasso

Basílica de Santa Maria del Mar

La Catedral

El Raval (p42)
The former port district includes a fabulous market, bars and restaurants, stunning art galleries and an unlikely Gaudi confection.

⊙ Top Sights

Mercat de la Boqueria

La Rambla & Barri Gòtic (p22)
Barcelona's old quarter combines famous La Rambla with narrow medieval streets and monumental buildings.

⊙ Top Sights

La Rambla

La Catedral

Explore
Barcelona

La Rambla & Barri Gòtic............. 22

El Raval 42

La Ribera &
Parc de la Ciutadella 54

Barceloneta & the Beaches......... 74

Passeig de Gràcia &
L'Eixample 86

Montjuïc, Poble Sec &
Sant Antoni.................................. 114

Camp Nou,
Pedralbes & Sarrià 132

Worth a Trip

La Sagrada Família 106
Village Life in Gràcia 110
Park Güell 112

La Barceloneta (p74)
MATT MUNRO/LONELY PLANET ©

Explore

La Rambla & Barri Gòtic

One of the world's most celebrated thoroughfares, La Rambla is an essential Barcelona experience. Crouched along its eastern flank, the Barri Gòtic (Gothic Quarter), which dates back to Roman times, is one of Barcelona's most rewarding bastions of tradition, where ancient monuments overlook pretty public squares that provide breathing space amid the wonderful tangle of laneways.

The Sights in a Day

☼ Start your day as early as possible with a stroll down **La Rambla** (p24), then head for **La Catedral** (p28); the sooner you get here after its 8am opening time (Monday to Saturday) the better. Depending on how long you linger, you probably have time for a morning visit to the **Museu Frederic Marès** (p34), punctuated by a coffee in its outdoor cafe.

☼ After a lunch of traditional Catalan cooking at **Cafè de l'Acadèmia** (p35), lose yourself in the labyrinth of the old quarter. The city's Roman heritage makes a fine theme on which to focus your meanderings, stopping in the **Museu d'Història de Barcelona** (p34) and passing by the **Temple Romà d'August** (p35). And on no account miss the **Església de Santa Maria del Pi** (p34).

✷ As night falls, **Plaça Reial** (p34) is a fine place to begin your evening, particularly at **Ocaña** (p38). After a meal at **Belmonte** (p36) or **Pla** (p36), catch a show at **Jamboree** (p41) or **Gran Teatre del Liceu** (p40). Dance the night away at **Marula Cafè** (p40), then end the day as you began: with a stroll down La Rambla.

For a local's day in the Barri Gòtic, see p30.

 Top Sights

La Rambla (p24)

La Catedral (p28)

🔍 **Local Life**

A Barri Gòtic Sunday (p30)

💗 **Best of Barcelona**

Catalan Food
Cafè de l'Acadèmia (p35)

Belmonte (p36)

Vinateria del Call (p36)

Allium (p38)

Bars
Ocaña (p38)

Sor Rita (p38)

Manchester (p40)

Oviso (p39)

Getting There

Ⓜ **Metro** This is the best option. Catalunya station (lines 1, 3, 6 and 7) sits at the top of La Rambla, Liceu (line 3) is at La Rambla's midpoint, while Jaume I (line 4) sits on the Barri Gòtic's eastern perimeter.

Ⓜ **Metro** Drassanes station (line 3) is at the waterfront end of La Rambla.

Top Sights
La Rambla

Everyone walks La Rambla during a Barcelona stay. In just a 1.25km strip you'll encounter food stalls, flower stands, street performers, grand public buildings, a pungent produce market, pickpockets, prostitutes and a veritable United Nations of passers-by. More than anywhere else this is where the city's passion for life as performance finds daily expression, as a relentless tide of people courses down towards the Mediterranean in a beguiling counterpoint to the static charms of Gaudí's architectural treasures.

Map p32, B5

Ⓜ Catalunya, Liceu or Drassanes

Aerial view of La Rambla

Don't Miss

La Font de Canaletes

From Plaça de Catalunya, La Rambla unfurls down the hill to the southeast. Its first manifestation, La Rambla de Canaletes, is named after the pretty 19th-century, wrought-iron fountain La Font de Canaletes. Local legend has it that anyone who drinks from its waters will return to Barcelona. More prosaically, delirious football fans gather here to celebrate whenever FC Barcelona wins.

Església de Betlem

A little further to the southeast, the early-18th-century **Església de Betlem** (La Rambla dels Estudis; ⊘9am-2pm & 6-9pm; Ⓜ Liceu) was once the most splendid of Barcelona's few baroque offerings. Its exterior still makes a powerful impression, but arsonists destroyed much of the interior at the outset of the Spanish Civil War in 1936. Approaching Christmas, check out the *pessebres* (nativity scenes).

Flower Stalls

La Rambla's assault on the senses continues along La Rambla de Sant Josep (named after a now-nonexistent monastery), which extends from Carrer de la Portaferrissa to Plaça de la Boqueria. For much of its length, La Rambla de les Flors (as it is popularly known) is lined with flower stalls, assailing passers-by with heady fragrances to accompany the gathering clamour.

Palau de la Virreina

The **Palau de la Virreina** is a grand 18th-century rococo mansion set back ever so slightly from La Rambla's western border. It houses the Centre de la Imatge, an avant-garde exhibition space with rotating shows that focus on cutting-edge photography.

☑ Top Tips

▶ Keep a close eye on your belongings at all times – pickpockets love La Rambla as much as tourists do.

▶ Take an early morning stroll and another late at night to sample La Rambla's many moods.

▶ Unless you're prepared to pay up to €10 for a beer, avoid the outdoor tables along the main thoroughfare.

▶ The balconies of the Museu de l'Eròtica have marvellous views of Mercat de la Boqueria's entrance.

✕ Take a Break

Want to sample Barcelona before the tourists arrived? Step into Cafè de L'Òpera (p40) for coffee and tapas.

With an impressive interior and a perfect people-watching terrace, detour to Ocaña (p38) for a coffee or a cocktail.

Mercat de la Boqueria

Restaurant chefs, homemakers, office workers and tourists all stroll amid the seemingly endless bounty of this hallowed market (p44). Discover glistening fruits and vegetables, gleaming fish counters, dangling smoked meats, pyramids of pungent cheeses, barrels full of olives and marinated peppers, and chocolate truffles and other sweets. Scattered about, a handful of popular tapas bars serve up delectable morsels.

Museu de l'Eròtica

Barcelona takes pride in being a pleasure centre and the **Museu de l'Eròtica** (Erotica Museum; ☎93 318 98 65; www.erotica-museum.com; La Rambla de Sant Josep 96; admission €9; ◷10am-midnight; ☎; ⓂLiceu), a private collection devoted to sex through the ages, falls somewhere between titillation, tawdriness and art. Exhibits range from exquisite *Kama Sutra* illustrations to early porn movies, S&M apparatus and a 2m wooden penis.

Mosaïc de Miró

A little further along lies an oft-overlooked mosaic by the great Catalan artist Joan Miró. The circular work imbedded in the pavement features his characteristically simple motifs in bold colours of blue, red and yellow. Miró himself chose the location for the mosaic, which lies not far from Passatge del Crèdit, where he was born.

Gran Teatre del Liceu

Built in 1847, destroyed by fire in 1994, and resurrected five years later, Barcelona's grand operatic stage, the **Gran Teatre del Liceu** (☏93 485 99 14; www.liceubarcelona.com; La Rambla dels Caputxins 51-59; tour 20/80min €5.50/11.50; ⏱guided tour 10am, short tour 11.30am, noon, 12.30pm & 1pm; Ⓜ Liceu) launched the careers of José Carreras and Montserrat Caballé. The marble staircase, Saló dels Miralls (Hall of Mirrors) and 19th-century stalls are original.

Plaça Reial

One of the loveliest squares in all of Barcelona, Plaça Reial is where many visitors divert from La Rambla and enter the city's Gothic Quarter, which shadows La Rambla from start to finish. A nightlife hub, popular meeting point and home to some modest early Gaudí structures, the square is a place you'll want to linger.

Plaça Reial (p34)

Centre d'Art Santa Mònica

Further south La Rambla gets seedier, widens out and changes its name to La Rambla de Santa Mònica. This stretch is named after the Convent de Santa Mònica, a monastery converted into an art gallery and cultural centre, the **Centre d'Art Santa Mònica** (☏93 567 11 10; www.artssantamonica.cat; La Rambla de Santa Mònica 7; admission free; ⏱11am-9pm Tue-Fri, 3-8pm Sat; Ⓜ Drassanes).

Museu de Cera

In a lane off La Rambla's eastern side, Barcelona's wax museum **Museu de Cera** (☏93 317 26 49; www.museocerabcn.com; Passatge de la Banca 7; adult/child €15/9; ⏱10am-10pm daily Jun-Sep, 10am-

2pm & 4-8pm Mon-Fri, 11am-2pm & 4.30-9pm Sat Oct-May; Ⓜ Drassanes) has more than 300 wax figures of familiar faces from around the world. There's everything from displays of twisted medieval torture to likenesses of Prince Charles and Camilla.

Mirador de Colom

Centuries after he stumbled across the Americas, Columbus (Colón in Spanish, Colom in Catalan) was honoured with the **Mirador de Colom** (☏93 302 52 24; Plaça del Portal de la Pau; lift adult/child €4.50/3; ⏱8.30am-8pm; Ⓜ Drassanes), a 60m-high monument built for the Universal Exhibition in 1888. Catch a lift to the top for a fine view down La Rambla.

Top Sights
La Catedral

For centuries the spiritual heart of Barcelona, La Catedral is a traditional counterweight to the avant-garde architectural flourishes of La Sagrada Família. Where Gaudí's flight of fancy speaks to the aspirations of a city intent on pushing the boundaries and embracing the future, Gothic La Catedral, at once lavish and sombre, anchors the city in its past. Begun in the late 13th century and not completed until six centuries later, the cathedral is Barcelona's history rendered in stone.

Map p32, C3

Plaça de la Seu

admission free, special visit €6, choir admission €2.80

⊙8am-12.45pm & 5.15-7.30pm Mon-Sat, special visit 1-5pm Mon-Sat, 2-5pm Sun & holidays

ⓜJaume I

Choir stalls, La Catedral

Don't Miss

Northwest Facade

From Plaça de la Seu, contemplate the richly decorated northwest facade. Although the cathedral was begun in 1298, the facade, based on a 1408 design, was not created until the 1870s. It reflects extravagant northern-European Gothic styles rather than the sparer Catalan version.

Sant Crist de Lepant

The main figure above the altar in the first chapel, to the right of the northwest entrance, is Sant Crist de Lepant. He was carried on the prow of the Spanish flagship at the Battle of Lepanto in 1571. It's said the figure acquired its odd stance by dodging an incoming cannonball.

Choir Stalls

In the heart of the main sanctuary – a soaring space divided into a central nave and two aisles by thin, elegant pillars – are the exquisitely sculpted, late-14th-century timber *coro* (choir stalls). The coats of arms belong to the Barcelona chapter of the Order of the Golden Fleece.

Crypt

The crypt beneath the main altar contains the remarkable alabaster tomb of the 4th-century Santa Eulàlia, one of Barcelona's patron saints; she suffered terrible tortures and finally death at the hands of the pagan Romans. Some of those gruesome tortures are depicted on the tomb.

Cloister

From the southwest transept, exit to the *claustre* (cloister), with its trees, fountains and geese (there have been geese here since medieval times). One of the chapels commemorates 930 priests, monks and nuns martyred in the Spanish Civil War.

☑ **Top Tips**

▶ Pay the €6 to visit in the afternoon; crowds are extraordinary during free admission periods.

▶ The €6 ticket also gives access to the choir stalls, Sala Capitular and the lift to the top of the spire.

▶ Return at night to see the floodlit northwest facade.

▶ If visiting during the period of free entry, arrive at 8am before the tour buses appear.

✘ **Take a Break**

No restaurants on Plaça de la Seu distinguish themselves, but the views from the outdoor tables are wonderful.

A short walk away to the southeast, the local favourite Cafè de l'Acadèmia (p35) serves excellent lunch specials by day, and tasty traditional dishes and wine in the evening.

Local Life
A Barri Gòtic Sunday

The Barri Gòtic can seem overrun by visitors at times, but it's on Sunday more than any other day that locals reclaim their neighbourhood, colonising the squares with small markets and frequenting places that few outsiders know about. Sunday is also the only day when the town hall – a Catalan icon – throws open its doors.

❶ Spiritual Start

Sunday mass remains an important part of life in the Barri Gòtic, so where better to begin than the 14th-century **Església de Sants Just i Pastor** (📞 93 301 74 33; www.basilicasantjust.cat; Plaça de Sant Just 5; ⏱11am-2pm & 5-8pm Mon-Sat, 10am-1pm Sun; Ⓜ Liceu or Jaume I)? This Gothic church holds a special place in Catalan hearts: on 11 September 1924, Gaudí was arrested here for refusing to speak Spanish to a policeman.

② Catalan Power

On Plaça de Sant Jaume, the **Palau de la Generalitat** (www.president.cat; Plaça de Sant Jaume; ⊘2nd & 4th weekend of month; MLiceu, Jaume I), the seat of Catalonia's regional government, was adapted from several Gothic mansions. The Saló de Sant Jordi (Hall of St George) is typical of the sumptuous interior. Visits must be booked online.

③ Town Hall Tour

Barcelona's town hall or **Ajuntament** (☏93 402 70 00; www.bcn.cat; Plaça de Sant Jaume; admission free; ⊘10.30am-1.30pm Sun; MLiceu, Jaume I) has been the seat of city power since the 14th century. It has a Catalan Gothic side facade, while its spectacular interior features a majestic staircase and the splendidly restored Saló de Cent (Chamber of the One Hundred).

④ Sardana

Catching a performance of *sardana*, the Catalan folk dance *par excellence,* is always a memorable event, at once an enjoyable spectacle and an important reassertion of Catalan identity. Your best chance is to turn up to Plaça Nova, next to La Catedral, at noon on Sundays (or 6.30pm on Saturdays), when performances usually take place.

⑤ Coins & Stamps

While much of Barcelona is still sleeping off the excesses of the night before, dedicated collectors make their way to the **Coin & Stamp Market** (Plaça Reial; ⊘9am-2.30pm Sun). Like all flea markets, it's always worth leafing through what's on offer in search of treasure, while some stallholders have branched out to sell a range of knick-knacks, both antique and otherwise.

⑥ Farmers & Painters

If it's the first or third Sunday of the month, make a beeline for Plaça del Pi and the **Farmers' Market** (⊘10am-9pm 1st & 3rd Fri-Sun), which draws vendors of fine cheeses, honeys and other artisan food products from around Catalonia. Around the corner, 50 local artists showcase their work in pretty **Plaça de Sant Josep Oriol** (⊘11am-8.30pm Sat, 10am-3pm Sun; MLiceu).

⑦ Sunday Lunch

Founded in 1786, **Can Culleretes** (☏93 317 30 22; www.culleretes.com; Carrer Quintana 5; mains €10-18; ⊘1.30-4pm Tue-Sun & 9-11pm Tue-Sat; MLiceu) is still going strong, with crowds flocking to enjoy its rambling interior, old-fashioned tile-filled decor, and enormous helpings of traditional Catalan food.

⑧ Chocolate con Churros

An afternoon favourite for Barcelonins, **Granja La Pallaresa** (Carrer de Petritxol 11; ⊘9am-1pm daily & 4-9pm Mon-Sat, 5-9pm Sun; MLiceu) serves up thick and rich hot chocolate. Order some crispy *churros* (*xurros* in Catalan; fried donut strips) for some delectable dunking.

C dels Carders

C d'en Giralt i Pellisser

C de Colomines

C dels Corders

C de la Bòria

C de la Princesa

C de l'Argenteria

Via Laietana

Plaça dels Traginers

CIUTAT VELLA

C de les Freixures

M Jaume I

Plaça de l'Angel

C del Sotstinent Navarro

C dels Lledó

C dels Mercaders

Museu d'Història de Barcelona

26

C de la Daguería

7

Plaça de Sant Just

10

12

LA RIBERA

Plaça de Ramon Berenguer el Gran

Plaça de Sant Iu

C de la Llibretería

1

6

C de Jaume I

Plaça de Sant Just

C del Palau

Plaça d'Antoni Maura

C de la Tapinería

Plaça de Sant Iu

Temple Romà d'August

Oficina d'Informació de Turisme de Barcelona

Plaça de Sant Miquel

C de Sant Pere més Baix

C dels Comtes

4

Museu Frederic Marès

Plaça de la Seu

C del Bisbe

Plaça de Sant Jaume

C del Pas de l'Enseyança

27

C de la Catedral

C de Sant Sever

La Catedral

Plaça Nova

13

C de la Fruita

C del Call

C Comtal

Plaça de Sant Felip Neri

Placeta de Manuel Ribé

8

5

Sinagoga Major

C dels Arcs

C de Ripoll

11

C dels Sagristans

25

C dels Banys Nous

24

C de Ferran

C de les Magdalenes

C de n'Amargós

14

C de Montsió

C d'en Bas

C Duran i Bas

Capellans

C dels Banys Nous

Plaça de Sant Josep Oriol

2

Església de Santa Maria del Pi

C del Pi

C de la Boquería

C d'en Rauric

Av del Portal de l'Angel

C de Santa Anna

C de la Canuda

Plaça de la Vila de Madrid

C de Bertrellans

C d'en Bot

C de la Portaferrissa

C del Pi

Plaça del Pi

BARRI GÒTIC

C del Petritxol

C d'en Roca

Plaça de la Boquería

Plaça de Ramon Amadeu

La Rambla de Canaletes

La Rambla dels Estudis

C d'en Bot

La Rambla

La Rambla de Sant Josep

C del Carme

Mercat de la Boquería

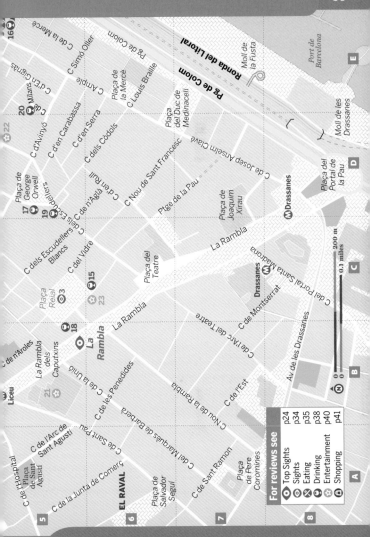

Port de Barcelona

Moll de la Fusta

Ronda del Litoral

Pg de Colom

Moll de les Drassanes

C de la Merce

C Simó Oller

Pg de Colom

16

C d'En Gignàs

C Ample

Plaça de la Mercè

C Louis Braille

20

Millans

C de

C d'Avinyó

C d'en Carabassa

C d'en Serra

C dels Còdols

Plaça del Duc de Medinaceli

22

Plaça del Portal de la Pau

Plaça de George Orwell

C Nou de Sant Francesc

C de Josep Anselm Clavé

17

C d'en Rull

C d'Avinyó

19

C dels Escudellers

Ptge de la Pau

Plaça de Joaquim Xirau

Drassanes

C dels Escudellers Blancs

C del Vidre

Plaça del Teatre

La Rambla

Drassanes

Plaça Reial

3

15

23

La Rambla

C del Portal Santa Madrona

C de Montserrat

C de l'Arc del Teatre

Av de les Drassanes

18

La Rambla

dels Caputxins

C de n'Aroles

La Rambla de la Unió

C de les Penedides

C de l'Est

Liceu

21

C de l'Arc de Sant Agustí

C de Sant Pau

C Nou de la Rambla

C de l'Hospital

Plaça de Sant Agustí

C del Marquès de Barberà

Plaça de Pere Coromines

C de la Junta de Comerç

EL RAVAL

C de Sant Ramon

Plaça de Salvador Seguí

200 m

0.1 miles

For reviews see

◉	Top Sights	p24
◉	Sights	p34
✖	Eating	p35
◑	Drinking	p38
✪	Entertainment	p40
🛍	Shopping	p41

Sights

Museu d'Història de Barcelona
MUSEUM

1 Map p32, D3

One of Barcelona's most fascinating museums takes you back through the centuries to the very foundations of Roman Barcino. Stroll over ruins of the old streets, sewers, laundries and factories that flourished here following the town's founding by Emperor Augustus around 10 BC. Equally impressive is the building itself, which was once part of the Palau Reial Major (Grand Royal Palace) on Plaça del Rei, among the key locations of medieval princely power in Barcelona. (☏ 93 256 21 00; www.museuhistoria.bcn.cat; Plaça del Rei; adult/child €7/free, free 1st Sun of month & 3-8pm Sun; ⊙ 10am-7pm Tue-Sat, 10am-8pm Sun; Ⓜ Jaume I)

Església de Santa Maria del Pi
CHURCH

2 Map p32, B4

This striking 14th-century church is a classic of Catalan Gothic, with an imposing facade, a wide interior and a single nave. The simple decor in the main sanctuary contrasts with the gilded chapels and exquisite stained-glass windows that bathe the interior in ethereal light. The beautiful rose window above its entrance is one of the world's largest. Occasional concerts are staged here (classical guitar, choral groups, chamber orchestras). (admission €5; ⊙ 10am-7pm Mon-Sat, 4-8pm Sun; Ⓜ Liceu)

Plaça Reial
SQUARE

3 Map p32, C5

One of the most photogenic squares in Barcelona, the Plaça Reial is a delightful retreat from the traffic and pedestrian mobs on the nearby Rambla. Numerous eateries, bars and nightspots lie beneath the arcades of 19th-century neoclassical buildings, with a buzz of activity at all hours. (Ⓜ Liceu)

Museu Frederic Marès
MUSEUM

4 Map p32, C2

A wild collection of historical curios lies inside this vast medieval complex, once part of the royal palace of Barcelona's counts. A rather worn coat of arms on the wall indicates that it was also once a seat of the Spanish Inquisition. Frederic Marès i Deulovol (1893–1991) was a wealthy sculptor, traveller and obsessive collector, and displays of religious art and vast varieties of bric-a-brac litter the museum. (☏ 93 256 35 00; www.museumares.bcn.es; Plaça de Sant Iu 5; admission €4.20, after 3pm Sun & 1st Sun of month free; ⊙ 10am-7pm Tue-Sat, 11am-8pm Sun; Ⓜ Jaume I)

Sinagoga Major
SYNAGOGUE

5 Map p32, C3

When an Argentine investor bought a run-down electrician's store with an eye to renovating it, he stumbled onto the remains of what could be the city's main medieval synagogue (some historians cast doubt on the claim). A guide will explain what is thought to be the significance of the site in various languages.

Plaça Reial

(📞 93 317 07 90; www.calldebarcelona.org; Carrer de Marlet 5; admission by suggested donation €2.50; 🕙 10.30am-6.30pm Mon-Fri, to 2.30pm Sat & Sun; Ⓜ Liceu)

Temple Romà d'August RUIN

6 ◎ Map p32, D3

Opposite the southeast end of La Catedral, narrow Carrer del Paradis leads towards Plaça de Sant Jaume. Inside No 10, itself an intriguing building with Gothic and baroque touches, are four columns and the architrave of Barcelona's main Roman temple, dedicated to Caesar Augustus and built to worship his imperial highness in the 1st century AD. (Carrer del Paradis 10; admission free; 🕙 10am-2pm Mon, to 7pm Tue-Sun; Ⓜ Jaume I)

Eating

Cafè de l'Acadèmia CATALAN $$

7 Map p32, D3

Expect a mix of traditional dishes with the occasional creative twist. At lunchtime, local *ajuntament* (town hall) office workers pounce on the *menú del día*. In the evening it is rather more romantic, as low lighting emphasises the intimacy of the timber ceiling and wooden decor. On warm days, you can also dine on the pretty square at the front. (📞 93 319 82 53; Carrer dels Lledó 1; mains €13-19; 🕙 1.30-4pm & 8.45-11.30pm Mon-Fri; Ⓜ Jaume I)

Top Tip

Roman Walls

The city's first architects of note were the Romans, who built a town here in the 1st century BC. Large relics of its 3rd- and 4th-century walls can still be seen in the Barri Gòtic, particularly at Plaça de Ramon Berenguer el Gran (D2) and by the northern end of Carrer del Sotstinent Navarro.

La Vinateria del Call   SPANISH $$

8 Map p32, C3

In a magical setting in the former Jewish quarter, this tiny jewelbox of a restaurant serves up tasty Iberian dishes including Galician octopus, cider-cooked chorizo and the Catalan *escalivada* (roasted peppers, aubergine and onions) with anchovies. Portions are small and made for sharing, and there's a good and affordable selection of wines. (📞 93 302 60 92; www.lavinateria delcall.com; Carrer de Sant Domènec del Call 9; small plates €7-12; ⏰ 7.30pm-1am; Ⓜ Jaume I)

Belmonte   TAPAS $$

9 Map p32, E5

This tiny tapas joint in the southern reaches of Barri Gòtic whips up beautifully prepared small plates – including an excellent *truita* (tortilla), rich *patatons a la sal* (salted baby potatoes with Romesco sauce) and tender *carpaccio de pop* (octopus carpaccio). Wash it down with the housemade *vermut* (vermouth). (📞 93 310 76 84; Carrer de la

Mercè 29; tapas €4-10; ⏰ 7pm-midnight Tue-Sat; Ⓜ Jaume I)

Pla   FUSION $$$

10 Map p32, D4

One of Gòtic's long-standing favourites, Pla is a stylish, romantically lit medieval dining room where the cooks churn out such temptations as oxtail braised in red wine, seared tuna with oven-roasted peppers, and polenta with seasonal mushrooms. It has a tasting menu for €38 Sunday to Thursday. (📞 93 412 65 52; www.elpla. cat; Carrer de la Bellafila 5; mains €18-25; ⏰ 7.30pm-midnight; 🖊; Ⓜ Jaume I)

Koy Shunka   JAPANESE $$$

11 Map p32, C1

Down a narrow lane north of the cathedral, Koy Shunka opens a portal to exquisite dishes from the East – mouthwatering sushi, sashimi, seared Wagyu beef and flavour-rich seaweed salads are served alongside inventive cooked fushion dishes like steamed clams with sake or tempura of scallops and king prawns with Japanese mushrooms. Don't miss the house speciality of tender *toro* (tuna belly). (📞 93 412 79 39; www.koyshunka.com; Carrer de Copons 7; multicourse menus €77-110; ⏰ 1.30-3pm Tue-Sun & 8.30-11pm Tue-Sat; Ⓜ Urquinaona)

Rasoterra   VEGETARIAN $

12 Map p32, D4

A delightful addition to the Gothic quarter, Rasoterra cooks up first-rate vegetarian dishes in a Zen-like setting

Understand

Growth of a City

The Romans were, in the 1st century BC, the first to build a lasting settlement on the plain where Barcelona now sprawls. The nucleus of their city, known as Barcino, lay within defensive walls whose outline roughly traced what is now the Barri Gòtic, a more-or-less standard rectangular Roman town. The forum lay approximately where Plaça de Sant Jaume is now and the whole city covered little more than 10 hectares.

In the centuries that followed, settlements spread beyond the city walls. By the 13th and 14th centuries, Barcelona was the capital of a growing Mediterranean empire with a rapidly growing population. Its walls were pushed outwards to enclose what we now know as El Raval and La Ribera; La Rambla (which takes its name from a seasonal stream, or *raml* in Arabic) lay outside the city walls until the 14th century.

By the mid-19th century, Barcelona was again bursting at the seams. The road between Barcelona and the then village of Gràcia was lined with trees in the 1820s, giving birth to the Passeig de Gràcia with gardens and fields on either side. The medieval walls were knocked down by 1856, and in 1869 work began on L'Eixample (the Extension, or Enlargement) to fill the open country between Barcelona and Gràcia.

Designed by Ildefons Cerdà, L'Eixample took the form of a grid with diamond-shaped intersections, broken up with gardens and parks and grafted onto the northern edge of the old town, starting at what is now Plaça de Catalunya.

The plan was revolutionary; until then it had been illegal to build on the plains, the area being a military zone. Building continued well into the 20th century. Well-to-do families snapped up prime plots and raised fanciful buildings in the eclectic style of the Modernistas. With restrictions no longer in place, Barcelona grew exponentially, swallowing up towns such as Gràcia, Sant Martí, Sants and Sant Andreu.

Top Tip

Menú del Día

One great way to cap prices on weekday lunches is to order the *menú del día*, which usually costs around €9 to €14. You'll be given a menu with five or six starters, the same number of mains and a handful of desserts – choose one of each.

with tall ceilings, low-playing jazz and fresh flowers on the tables. The creative, globally influenced menu changes regularly and might feature Vietnamese-style coconut pancakes with tofu and vegetables, beluga lentils with basmati rice, and pear and goat cheese quesadillas. Good vegan and gluten-free options. (📞93 318 69 26; Carrer del Palau 5; tapas €5-8, lunch specials €7-10; ⏱noon-5pm Tue, to midnight Wed-Sun; 🍴; Ⓜ Jaume I)

Allium   CATALAN, FUSION $$

14   Map p32, C4

This inviting newcomer to Barri Gòtic serves beautifully prepared tapas dishes and changing specials (including seafood paella for one). The menu, which changes every two or threee weeks, focuses on seasonal, organic cuisine. Its bright, modern interior sets it apart from other neighbourhood options; it's also open continuously, making it a good bet for those who don't want to wait until 9pm for a meal. (📞93 302 30 03; Carrer del Call 17; mains €8-16; ⏱noon-4pm Mon-Tue, to 10.30pm Wed-Sat; Ⓜ Liceu)

Els Quatre Gats   CATALAN $$$

14   Map p32, B1

Once the lair of Barcelona's *modernista* artists, Els Quatre Gats exudes charm with its colourful tile and timberwork (and portraits of some of its former customers). To sample the atmosphere, a drink in the bar will suffice. Otherwise head out to the rear dining courtyard, where the 1st-floor verandah is the ideal spot to enjoy standard Catalan fare. (📞93 302 41 40; Carrer de Montsió 3; meals: €30-40; ⏱8am-2am; Ⓜ Urquinaona)

Drinking

Ocaña   BAR

15 🍺 Map p32, C6

Named after a flamboyant artist who once lived on Plaça Reial, Ocaña is a beautifully designed space with fluted columns, stone walls, candlelit chandeliers and plush furnishings. Have a seat on the terrace and watch the passing people parade, or head downstairs to the Moorish-inspired Apotheke bar or the chic lounge a few steps away, where DJs spin for a mix of beauties and bohemians on weekend nights. (📞93 676 48 14; www.ocana.cat; Plaça Reial 13; ⏱5pm-2.30am Mon-Fri, from 11am Sat & Sun; Ⓜ Liceu)

Sor Rita   BAR

16 🍺 Map p32, E5

Full of all things kitsch, Sor Rita is pure eye candy, from its leopard-print wall-

Barri Gòtic cafe

paper to its high-heel festooned ceiling, and decorations inspired by the films of Almodóvar. It's a fun and festive scene, with special-event nights throughout the week, including tarot readings on Mondays, €5 all-you-can-eat snack buffets on Tuesdays, karaoke Wednesdays and gin specials on Thursdays. (Carrer de la Mercè 27; ⏰7pm-2.30am; Ⓜ Jaume I)

Oviso   BAR

17 Ⓟ Map p32, D5

Oviso is a popular budget-friendly restaurant with outdoor tables on the plaza, but shows its true bohemian colours by night, with a mixed crowd, a rock-and-roll vibe and a rustic decorated two-room interior plastered with curious murals – geese taking flight, leaping dolphins and blue peacocks framing the brightly painted concrete walls. (Carrer d'Arai 5; ⏰10am-2.30am; 📶; Ⓜ Liceu)

Barcelona Pipa Club   BAR

18 Ⓟ Map p32, B5

This pipe-smokers' club is like an apartment, with all sorts of interconnecting rooms and knick-knacks – notably the pipes after which the place is named. Buzz at the door and head two floors up. Note there's no longer any smoking here, though there is occasional live music. (📞93 302 47 32; www.bpipaclub.com; Plaça Reial 3; ⏰10pm-4am; Ⓜ Liceu)

Barri Gòtic Cafes

Some of Barcelona's most atmospheric cafes lie hidden in the old cobbled lanes of Barri Gòtic.

Salterio (Map p32, C3; Carrer de Sant Domènec del Call 4; 2pm-midnight; Jaume I) serves teas and *sardo* (grilled flat-bread pizzas) amid stone walls and ambient Middle Eastern music.

Nearby, **Čaj Chai** (Map p32, C3; 93 301 95 92; www.cajchai.com; Carrer de Sant Domènec del Call 12; 3-10pm Mon, 10.30am-10pm Tue-Sun; Jaume I) is a bright and buzzing tearoom with numerous teas on offer.

Going strong since 1929, the elegant **Cafè de l'Òpera** (Map p32, B5; 93 317 75 85; www.cafeoperabcn.com; La Rambla 74; 8.30am-2.30am; Liceu) is La Rambla's most intriguing snack spot.

Marula Cafè

BAR

 19   Map p32, D5

A fantastic funk find in the heart of the Barri Gòtic, Marula will transport you to the 1970s and the best in funk and soul. James Brown fans will think they've died and gone to heaven. It's not, however, a monothematic place and DJs slip in other tunes, from breakbeat to house. Samba and other Brazilian dance sounds also penetrate here. (www.marulacafe.com; Carrer dels Escudellers 49; 11pm-5am Wed-Sun; Liceu)

Manchester

BAR

20   Map p32, E5

A drinking den that has undergone several transformations over the years now treats you to the sounds of great Manchester bands, from Joy Division to Oasis, but probably not the Hollies. It has a pleasing rough-and-tumble feel, with tables jammed in every which way. (www.manchesterbar.com; Carrer de Milans 5; 7pm-2.30am; Liceu)

Entertainment

Gran Teatre del Liceu

THEATRE, LIVE MUSIC

21   Map p32, B5

Barcelona's grand old opera house, restored after fire in 1994, is one of the most technologically advanced theatres in the world. To take up a seat in the grand auditorium, returned to all its 19th-century glory but with the very latest in acoustic accoutrements, is to be transported to another age. Tickets can cost anything from €9 for a cheap seat behind a pillar to €205 for a well-positioned night at the opera. (93 485 99 00; www.liceubarcelona.com; La Rambla dels Caputxins 51-59; box office 1.30-8pm Mon-Fri & 1hr before show Sat & Sun; Liceu)

Harlem Jazz Club

JAZZ

22   Map p32, D5

This narrow, old-city dive is one of the best spots in town for jazz, as well as funk, Latin, blues and gypsy jazz. It attracts a mixed crowd which maintains a respectful silence during the acts. Most concerts start around 10pm. Get in early if you want a seat in front of the stage. (☑93 310 07 55; www. harlemjazzclub.es; Carrer de la Comtessa de Sobradiel 8; admission around €7-8; ⊙8pm-5am Tue-Sat; MDrassanes)

Jamboree   LIVE MUSIC

23 ⭐ Map p32, C6

For over half a century, Jamboree has been offering high-calibre acts featuring jazz trios, blues, Afrobeats, Latin music and big-band sounds. Two concerts are held most nights (at 8pm and 10pm), after which Jamboree morphs into a DJ-spinning club at midnight. WTF jam sessions are held Mondays (entrance a mere €5). Buy tickets online to save a few euros. (☑93 319 17 89; www.masimas. com/jamboree; Plaça Reial 17; admission €10-20; ⊙8pm-6am; MLiceu)

Shopping

Empremtes de Catalunya   HANDICRAFTS

24 🔒 Map p32, C4

A celebration of Catalan products, this nicely designed store is a great place to browse for unique gifts. You'll find jewellery with designs inspired by Roman iconography, works that reference Gaudí and Barcelona's Gothic era, plus pottery, wooden toys, silk scarves, notebooks, housewares and more. (☑93 467 46 60; Carrer dels Banys Nous 11; ⊙10am-8pm Mon-Sat, to 2pm Sun; MLiceu)

Caelum   FOOD & DRINK

25 🔒 Map p32, B3

Carefully prepared sweets and other goods that have been the pride of Spanish convents through the centuries arrive here from all corners of Spain. Tempting traditional items include sticky marzipan and olive oil with thyme. Take a seat at a huddle of tables upstairs or head downstairs to what was once a medieval Jewish bathhouse. (Carrer de la Palla 8; ⊙10.30am-8.30pm Mon-Thu, 11am-11pm Fri & Sat, 11.30am-9pm Sun; MLiceu)

Fires, Festes i Tradicions   FOOD, DRINK

26 🔒 Map p32, D3

Whether assembling a picnic or looking for edible mementos, don't miss this little shop, which stocks a wide range of specialities from Catalunya, including jams, sausages and cheeses. (☑93 269 12 61; Carrer de la Dagueria 13; ⊙4-8.30pm Mon, 10am-8.30pm Tue-Sat; MJaume I)

La Manual Alpargatera   SHOES

27 🔒 Map p32, C4

Everyone from Salvador Dalí to Jean Paul Gaultier has ordered a pair of *espadrilles* (rope-soled canvas shoes or sandals) from this famous store, which is the birthplace of the iconic footware. The shop was founded just after the Spanish Civil War, though the roots of the simple shoe design date back thousands of years. (☑93 301 01 72; lamanualalpargatera.es; Carrer d'Avinyó 7; ⊙9.30am-1.30pm & 4.30-8pm; MLiceu)

Explore

El Raval

Long one of the most rough-and-tumble parts of Barcelona, El Raval is now undeniably hip in a grungy, inner-city way. Attractions here include the Mercat de la Boqueria, two stunning centres for contemporary arts and lively streets dotted with colourful shops, eateries and cafes. Night-time is El Raval's forte, with its mix of eccentric, trendy and downright ancient bars and clubs.

The Sights in a Day

☀ The **Mercat de la Boqueria** (p44) ranks among the most enduring of Barcelona institutions and it's at its best in the morning; we recommend at least a couple of hours here. Leave behind the cries of fishmongers and make your way to the **Museu d'Art Contemporani de Barcelona** (p49) to sample the cutting edge of contemporary art.

☀ After a pre-lunch *aperitivo* at **Elisabets** (p47) and a sit-down lunch at **Caravelle** (p50), take in an exhibition or two at the **Centre de Cultura Contemporània de Barcelona** (p50). Head south, via Barcelona's favourite milk bar, **Granja M Viader** (p47), to the old city's only Gaudí masterpiece, **Palau Güell** (p49), then continue on to **Església de Sant Pau del Camp** (p50), one of Barcelona's most tranquil churches.

☽ Start off the evening with a show at **Jazz Sí Club** (p47), followed by dinner at celebrated **Suculent** (p51). Afterwards take in El Raval's nightlife at vintage drinking spots like **Bar Marsella** (p47), **Casa Almirall** (p52) or **Boadas** (p51).

For a local's day in El Raval, see p46.

⊙ Top Sights

Mercat de la Boqueria (p44)

◯ Local Life

Revelling in El Raval (p46)

♥ Best of Barcelona

Contemporary Art & Architecture

Museu d'Art Contemporani de Barcelona (p49)

Centre de Cultura Contemporània de Barcelona (p50)

Palau Güell (p49)

Catalan Cooking

Suculent (p51)

Mam i Teca (p50)

Mercat de la Boqueria (p44)

Elisabets (p47)

Getting There

 Metro Your best transport option. Catalunya (lines 1, 3, 6 and 7) and Universitat (lines 1 and 2) sit at the neighbourhood's northern end, while Liceu (line 3) occupies the midpoint, on La Rambla to the east.

Ⓜ **Metro** Drassanes (line 3), Paral·lel (lines 2 and 3) and Sant Antoni (line 2) are good for southern El Raval.

Top Sights
Mercat de la Boqueria

Barcelona's most agreeable sensory experience is found at its central market. Completed in 1914 with a Modernisme-influenced design, this is one Barcelona landmark where the architecture is overshadowed by what lies within – the freshest produce from around Spain, the evocative starting point of many a memorable Barcelona meal, and a hum of activity unlike anywhere else in the city. Wander to get lost. Marvel at the sheer variety. And then sit back to watch from a bar stool.

Map p48, C3

☎ 93 318 25 84

www.boqueria.info

La Rambla 91

🕒 8am-8.30pm Mon-Sat, closed Sun

Ⓜ Liceu

Juice and produce stall, Mercat de la Boqueria

Don't Miss

Fish Market

While stalls aimed at tourists make tentative in-roads, the fish market in the market's geographical centre is the guardian of tradition. Razor clams and red prawns, salmon, sea bass and swordfish, it's all as fresh as when it was caught; so much so that there's scarcely a fishy aroma to inhale. Barcelona's love affair with fish and seafood starts here.

Juanito at Bar Pinotxo

As one respected Barcelona food critic described him, Juanito is 'the true spirit of the market'. Head barman at Bar Pinotxo (p51) for more than four decades, resplendent in waistcoat and bow tie, and unfailingly warm in many languages and none, he cajoles his staff, greets passers-by and announces the daily specials in the finest Barcelona tradition of food as performance.

El Llar del Pernil

The family-run **Joan La Llar del Pernil** (⊙8am-3pm Mon-Thu, to 8pm Fri & Sat) is our pick of the numerous purveyors of *jamón* (cured Spanish-style ham; *pernil* in Catalan) scattered around the market. Stall owner Joan knows his *jamón*, cheerfully regaling passers-by with lessons in the dark arts of cured meats as he cuts another wafer-thin slice and hands it over to try.

El Quim

The food at **El Quim** (⊙7am-4pm Tue-Thu, to 5pm Fri & Sat), buried in the heart of the market, is as fresh as the market produce. It offers a dazzling array of dishes, but does particularly wonderful things with eggs: *tortilla de patatas* (Spanish omelette), fried eggs with squid, or with foie gras... Pull up a stool.

☑ **Top Tips**

▶ The market is closed on Sunday.

▶ Many stalls, including most of those selling fish, are closed on Monday.

▶ The market's stallholders are among the world's most photographed – ask permission before taking pictures and where possible buy something from their stall.

▶ Gather food from your favourite stalls with a picnic in mind – having a foodie purpose brings a whole new dimension to your market experience.

✖ **Take a Break**

For market-fresh food and some of the market's best cooking, pull up a stool at El Quim.

To soak up the clamour from a front-row vantage point, stop by Bar Pinotxo (p51).

Local Life
Revelling in El Raval

El Raval is a neighbourhood whose contradictory impulses are legion. This journey through the local life of the *barrio* takes you from haunts beloved by the savvy young professionals moving into the area to gritty streetscapes and one-time slums frequented by Barcelona's immigrants and street-walkers. En route, we stop at places that, unlike the rest of the neighbourhood, haven't changed in decades.

❶ A Neighbourhood Square
For a slice of local life, the Plaça de Vicenç Martorell is difficult to beat. It's where the locals come to play with their kids or read the newspapers over a coffee or wine at **Bar Kasparo** (Plaça de Vicenç Martorell 4; ⏰9am-10pm; Ⓜ Catalunya). Just a short hop from La Rambla, this is Barcelona as locals live it.

❷ Musical Browsing

Carrer dels Tallers was once lined with music shops. Sadly, the economic crisis took its toll and now only **Discos Castelló** (Carrer dels Tallers 7; ⏰10am-8.30pm Mon-Sat; Ⓜ Catalunya) remains, selling new and secondhand CDs and vinyl of all types, along with a selection of related books and paraphernalia.

❸ Home-Style Cooking

Northern El Raval is rapidly gentrifying, but places like **Elisabets** (☎93 317 58 26; Carrer d'Elisabets 2-4; mains €8-10; ⏰7.30am-11pm Mon-Thu & Sat, until 2am Fri, closed Aug; Ⓜ Catalunya) hold firm. The walls are lined with old radio sets and the lunch menu varies daily. If you prefer à la carte, try the *ragú de jabalí* (wild boar stew) and finish with *mel i mató* (a Catalan dessert made from cheese and honey).

❹ Homemade Hot Chocolate

The fifth generation of its founding family runs **Granja M Viader** (☎93 318 34 86; www.granjaviader.cat; Carrer d'en Xuclà 6; ⏰9am-1.30pm & 5-9pm Mon-Sat; Ⓜ Liceu), an atmospheric milk bar and cafe established in 1873. This place invented *cacaolat,* the chocolate-and-skimmed-milk drink now popular all over Spain. Try a cup of homemade hot chocolate and whipped cream (ask for a *suís*).

❺ Preloved Shopping

Looking for fashion bargains that are perfect for passing unnoticed in this 'hood? In little more than 100m along **Carrer de la Riera Baixa**, from Carrer del Carme to Carrer de l'Hospital, you'll find nearly a dozen clothes shops, mostly selling secondhand.

❻ Live Music

Run by the Taller de Músics (Musicians' Workshop), the tiny **Jazz Sí Club** (☎93 329 00 20; www.tallerdemusics.com; Carrer de Requesens 2; admission incl drink €4-9; ⏰8.30-11pm Tue-Sat, 6.30-10pm Sun; Ⓜ Sant Antoni) hosts a varied gig program from jazz jams through to some good flamenco (Friday nights). Thursday night is Cuban night. Concerts start early (between 6.30pm and 8.45pm), but arrive early to get a good spot.

❼ Scenic Stroll

For a wide cross-section of the neighbourhood's multicultural mix, take a stroll down the palm-lined **Rambla del Raval**. Flanked by restaurants and outdoor cafes, this promenade is Barcelona's newest rambla (laid out in 1995). Don't miss the enormous, whiskered *Gat* (Cat) sculpture by Colombian artist Fernando Botero, a favourite meeting spot in Raval.

❽ Absinthe, Anyone?

End the day at **Bar Marsella** (Carrer de Sant Pau 65; ⏰10pm-2.30am Mon-Wed, 10pm-3am Thu-Sat; Ⓜ Liceu), which opened in 1820 and has barely changed since; assorted chandeliers, tiles and mirrors decorate its one rambunctious room. As in Hemingway's time, absinthe is the drink of choice, which should give you a warm glow – though treat this potent libation with respect!

A

Universitat de Barcelona

1

Gran Via de les Corts Catalanes

Ronda de la Universitat

Plaça de la Universitat

Ⓜ Universitat

C de Pelai

C dels Tallers

Centre de Cultura Contemporània de Barcelona

2

Plaça de Terenci Moix

16 🛇 C de Validzella

3 🛇 C de Montalegre

2 🛇 MACBA

Plaça dels Àngels

C del Tigre

C del Lleo C de Joaquín Costa

11 🛇 C de la Lluna

Plaça del Pes de la Palla

3

5 🛇 13 🛇

C de la Riera Alta

C del Carme

Ronda de Sant Antoni

Plaça del Padró

C de l'Hospital

7 🛇

Ⓜ❌ Sant Antoni

Ronda de Sant Pau

4

C de la Cera

C de l'Aurora

Rambla del Raval

EL RAVAL

C de les Carretes

C de la Reina Amàlia

C de la Riereta

Plaça de Salvador Seguí

8

SANT ANTONI

Plaça de Josep Maria Folch i Torres

Església de Sant Pau del Camp

🛇 4

12 🛇

5

For reviews see
🛇	Top Sights	p44
🛇	Sights	p49
❌	Eating	p50
🍷	Drinking	p51
🛍	Shopping	p53

Ⓜ Paral·lel

B

Ⓜ Catalunya

Plaça de Catalunya

C de Fontanella

ⓘ Oficina d'Informació de Turisme de Barcelona

C de Bergara

Ⓜ Catalunya

La Rambla de Canaletes

C de Santa Anna

Plaça de Vicenç Martorell

10 La Rambla dels Estudis

17 🛇

C del Pintor Fortuny

C dels Àngels

6 🛇

Mercat de 🛇 la Boqueria

La Rambla de Sant Josep

9 ❌

C de la Junta de Comerç

C de Sant Pau

C del Marquès de Barberà

C

C de la Canuda

Plaça de la Vila de Madrid

C de Montsió

C de la Portaferrissa

La Rambla de Sant Josep

Plaça de Sant Josep Oriol

Ⓜ Liceu

La Rambla

C de la Boqueria

Plaça Reial

La Rambla dels Caputxins

1 🛇 Palau Güell

C de l'Est

14 🍷

15 🍷 La Rambla de Santa Mònica

Av de les Drassanes

C de les Tàpies

C Nou de la Rambla

C de l'Om

C de l'Arc del Teatre

Av del Paral·lel

Parc de les Tres Xemeneies

D

0 ———— 200 m
0 ———— 0.1 miles

Ⓜ Urquinaona

Via Laietana

LA RIBERA

C Comtal

Plaça d'Antoni Maura

BARRI GÒTIC

Plaça de la Seu

Plaça Nova

C de la Palla

C del Bisbe

Plaça de Sant Jaume

C del Call

CIUTAT VELLA

C de Ferran

C d'Avinyó

C dels Escudellers

Plaça del Teatre

Ⓜ Drassanes

Plaça del Portal de la Pau

MACBA

Sights

Palau Güell

PALACE

1 ◉ Map p48, D4

Finally reopened in its entirety in May 2012 after several years of refurbishment, this is a magnificent example of the early days of Gaudí's fevered architectural imagination – the extraordinary neo-Gothic mansion, one of the few major buildings of that era raised in Ciutat Vella, gives an insight into its maker's prodigious genius. (☎93 472 57 75; www.palauguell.cat; Carrer Nou de la Rambla 3-5; adult/concession €12/8; ⏱10am-8pm Tue-Sun; Ⓜ Drassanes)

MACBA

MUSEUM

2 ◉ Map p48, B2

Designed by Richard Meier, MACBA has become the city's foremost contemporary art centre, with captivating exhibitions for the serious art lover. The permanent collection on the ground floor dedicates itself to Spanish and Catalan art from the second half of the 20th century, with works by Antoni Tàpies, Joan Brossa and Miquel Barceló, though international artists such as Paul Klee, Bruce Nauman and John Cage are also represented. (Museu d'Art Contemporani de Barcelona; ☎93 412 08 10; www.macba.cat; Plaça dels Àngels 1; adult/concession €10/8; ⏱11am-7.30pm Mon & Wed-Fri, 10am-9pm Sat, 10am-3pm Sun & holidays; Ⓜ Universitat)

Centre de Cultura Contemporània de Barcelona
CULTURAL BUILDING

3 Map p48, B2

A complex of auditoriums, exhibition spaces and conference halls opened here in 1994 in what had been an 18th-century hospice, the Casa de la Caritat. The courtyard, with a vast glass wall on one side, is spectacular. The centre hosts a constantly changing program of exhibitions, film cycles and other events. (CCCB; ☎ 93 306 41 00; www.cccb.org; Carrer de Montalegre 5; 2 exhibitions adult/ senior & student/child under 16yr €8/6/free, 1 exhibition €6/4/free, free on Sun 3-8pm; ⏲ 11am-8pm Tue-Sun; M Universitat)

 Top Tip

ArticketBCN

Barcelona's best bargain for art lovers is the **ArticketBCN** (www.articketbcn.org; per person €30), which gives you entry to six museums for less than half of what you'd pay if you bought individual tickets. The six museums are the Museu d'Art Contemporani de Barcelona, the Centre de Cultura Contemporània de Barcelona, the Museu Nacional d'Art de Catalunya, Fundació Joan Miró, Fundació Antoni Tàpies and the Museu Picasso. The ArticketBCN can be purchased at all participating museums or online at www.barcelonaturisme.com or www.telentrada.com.

Església de Sant Pau del Camp
CHURCH

4 Map p48, B5

The best example of Romanesque architecture in the city is the dainty little cloister of this church. Set in a somewhat dusty garden, the 12th-century church also boasts some Visigothic sculptural detail on the main entrance. (Carrer de Sant Pau 101; adult/concession €3/2; ⏲ 10am-1.30pm & 4-7.30pm Mon-Sat; M Paral·lel)

Eating

Mam i Teca
CATALAN $$

5 Map p48, B3

A tiny place with half a dozen tables, Mam i Teca is as much a lifestyle choice as a restaurant. Locals drop in and hang about at the bar, and diners are treated to Catalan dishes made with locally sourced products and adhering to Slow Food principles. Try, for example, cod fried in olive oil with garlic and red pepper, or pork ribs with chickpeas. (☎ 93 441 33 35; Carrer de la Lluna 4; mains €9-12; ⏲ 1-4pm & 8pm-midnight Mon, Wed-Fri & Sun, closed Sat lunch; M Sant Antoni)

Caravelle
INTERNATIONAL $$

6 Map p48, B3

A bright little joint, beloved of the hipsters of the Raval and anyone with a discerning palate. Tacos as you've never tasted them (cod, lime alioli and radish; pulled pork with roast corn and avocado), a superior steak sandwich on homemade brioche with pickled celeriac and all manner of soul food. Drinks are every bit as inventive – try the homemade ginger beer or grapefruit soda. (☑93 317 98 92; Carrer del Pintor Fortuny 31; mains €10-13; ⏱8.30am-6.30pm Mon-Wed, 8.30am-1am Thu, 10.30am-1am Sat, 10.30am-6.30pm Sun; Ⓜ Liceu)

Sésamo
VEGETARIAN $

7 Map p48, A4

Widely held to be the best vegie restaurant in the city, Sésamo is a cosy, fun place. The menu is mostly tapas, and most people go for the seven-course tapas menu (wine included; €25), but there are a few more substantial dishes. Nice touches include the home-baked bread and cakes. (☑93 441 64 11; Carrer de Sant Antoni Abat 52; tapas €6; ⏱8pm-midnight Tue-Sun; ✈; Ⓜ Sant Antoni)

Suculent
CATALAN $$

8 Map p48, C4

Michelin-starred chef Carles Abellan (of Comerç 24 fame) adds to his stable with this old-style bistro, which showcases the best of Catalan cuisine. From the cod brandade to the oxtail stew with truffled sweet potato, only the best ingredients are used, so be warned that the prices can mount up a bit, but this is a great place to sample the regional highlights. (☑93 443 65 79; www.suculent.com; Rambla del Raval 39; mains €11-20; ⏱1-4pm & 8.30-11.30pm Wed-Sun, closed Sun night; Ⓜ Liceu)

Bar Pinotxo
TAPAS $$

9 Map p48, C3

Bar Pinotxo is arguably La Boqueria's, and even Barcelona's, best tapas bar. It sits among the half-dozen or so informal eateries within the market, and the popular owner, Juanito, might serve up chickpeas with a sweet sauce of pine nuts and raisins, a fantastically soft mix of potato and spinach sprinkled with coarse salt, baby-soft baby squid with cannellini beans, or a quivering cube of caramel-sweet pork belly. (www.pinotxobar.com; Mercat de la Boqueria; mains €8-15; ⏱6am-4pm Mon-Sat; Ⓜ Liceu)

Drinking

Boadas
COCKTAIL BAR

10 Map p48, C2

One of the city's oldest cocktail bars, Boadas is famed for its daiquiris.

Local Life
Medieval Intrigue

Gaudí died at the 15th-century **Antic Hospital de la Santa Creu** (Map 48, B3; Former Hospital of the Holy Cross; ☎93 270 16 21; www.bnc.cat; Carrer de l'Hospital 56; admission free; ⏰9am-8pm Mon-Fri, to 2pm Sat; Ⓜ Liceu), which now houses Catalonia's national library, an arts school and the Institute for Catalan Studies. Visit the grand reading rooms beneath broad Gothic stone arches, where you'll also find temporary exhibitions. Its delightful, if somewhat frayed, colonnaded courtyard has a popular cafe.

Bow-tied waiters have been serving up unique drinkable creations since Miguel Boadas opened it in 1933; in fact Miró and Hemingway both drank here. Miguel was born in Havana, where he was the first barman at the immortal La Floridita. (www.boadascocktails.com; Carrer dels Tallers 1; ⏰noon-2am Mon-Thu, noon-3am Fri & Sat; Ⓜ Catalunya)

Casa Almirall   BAR

11   Map p48, A3

In business since the 1860s, this dark and intriguing corner bar has Modernista decor and a mixed clientele. There are some great original pieces in here, like the marble counter, and the cast-iron statue of the muse of the Universal Exposition, held in Barcelona in 1888. (www.casaalmirall.com; Carrer de Joaquín Costa 33; ⏰6pm-2.30am Mon-Thu, 6.30-3am Fri, noon-3am Sat, noon-1.30am Sun; Ⓜ Universitat)

La Confitería   BAR

12 🚇 Map p48, B5

This is a trip into the 19th century. Until the 1980s it was a confectioner's shop, and although the original cabinets are now lined with booze, the look of the place has barely changed in its conversion into a laid-back bar. A quiet enough spot for a house *vermut* (€3; add your own soda) in the early evening, it fills with theatregoers and local partiers later at night. (Carrer de Sant Pau 128; ⏰7.30pm-3am Mon-Thu, 1pm-3am Fri-Sun; Ⓜ Paral·lel)

Marmalade   BAR

13 🚇 Map p48, B3

The golden hues of this backlit bar and restaurant beckon seductively through the glass facade. There are various distinct spaces, decorated in different but equally sumptuous styles, and a pool table next to the bar. Cocktails are big business here, and a selection of them are €5 all night. (www.marmaladebarcelona.com; Carrer de la Riera Alta 4-6; ⏰6.30pm-2.30am Mon-Wed, 10am-2.30am Thu-Sun; Ⓜ Sant Antoni)

Moog   CLUB

14 🚇 Map p48, D4

This fun and minuscule club is a standing favourite with the downtown crowd. In the main dance area, DJs dish out house, techno and electro, while upstairs you can groove to a nice blend of indie and occasional classic-pop throwbacks. (www.masimas.com/moog; Carrer de l'Arc del Teatre 3; admission €10; ⏰midnight-5am Mon-Thu & Sun, midnight-6am Fri & Sat; Ⓜ️Drassanes)

Bar Pastís   BAR

15 🍷 Map p48, D4

A French cabaret theme (with lots of Piaf in the background) dominates this tiny, cluttered classic. It's been going, on and off, since the end of WWII. You'll need to be in here before 9pm to have a hope of sitting, getting near the bar or anything much else. On some nights it features live acts, usually performing French *chansons*. (www.barpastis.com; Carrer de Santa Mònica 4; ⏰7.30pm-2am daily; Ⓜ️Drassanes)

Shopping

Fantastik   ARTS & CRAFTS

16 🔒 Map p48, A2

Over 400 products, including a Mexican skull rattle, robot moon explorer from China and recycled plastic zebras from South Africa, are to be found in this colourful shop, which sources its items from Mexico, India, Bulgaria, Russia, Senegal and 20 other countries. It's a perfect place to buy all the things you don't need but can't live without. (www.fantastik.es; Carrer de Joaquín Costa 62; ⏰11am-2pm & 4-8.30pm Mon-Fri, noon-9pm Sat, closed Sun; Ⓜ️Universitat)

MICHAEL HEFFERNAN/LONELY PLANET ©

Boadas (p51)

La Portorriqueña   COFFEE

17 🔒 Map p48, B2

Coffee beans from around the world, freshly ground before your eyes, has been the winning formula in this store since 1902. It also offers all sorts of chocolate goodies. The street is good for little old-fashioned food boutiques. (Carrer d'en Xuclà 25; ⏰9am-2pm & 5-8pm Mon-Fri, 9am-2pm Sat; Ⓜ️Catalunya)

Explore

La Ribera & Parc de la Ciutadella

In La Ribera is one of Barcelona's most beguiling corners: El Born. The old town's epicentre in medieval times, leafy Passeig del Born is again abuzz, crammed with bars, restaurants and boutiques. Adding to the neighbourhood's appeal, La Ribera also boasts the Museu Picasso, Barcelona's mightiest Gothic church, a wonderful market and the largest park in downtown Barcelona.

The Sights in a Day

In a bid to avoid the crowds, get to the **Museu Picasso** (p56) early, then take a guided tour of the **Palau de la Música Catalana** (p66) to fully appreciate the genius and eccentricity of Modernisme. The **Mercat de Santa Caterina** (p66) is perfect for stocking up for a picnic lunch in the **Parc de la Ciutadella** (p66).

Explore the park after lunch, then head to the **Museu de la Xocolata** (p67) for dessert. After such sinful pleasures, settle into a pew to admire the grace and splendour of the **Basílica de Santa Maria del Mar** (p60). The church is just as beautiful on the outside, so make for our favourite vantage point, **La Vinya del Senyor** (p71), until evening falls.

The dining options in El Born are limitless, but we'd start with tapas at convivial **Cal Pep** (p69), followed by creative global dishes at **El Atril** (p69), leaving room for the decadent cuisine at **Comerç 24** (p69). After dinner, enjoy a nightcap at laid-back **Rubí** (p71).

For a local's night out in El Born, see p62.

👁 Top Sights

Museu Picasso (p56)

Basílica de Santa Maria del Mar (p60)

🔍 Local Life

Tapas & Bar Hopping in El Born (p62)

💙 Best of Barcelona

Tapas

Bormuth (p63)

El Xampanyet (p63)

Comerç 24 (p69)

Cal Pep (p69)

Euskal Etxea (p63)

Bar del Pla (p63)

La Llavor dels Orígens (p70)

Wine & Cocktail Bars

Juanra Falces (p71)

Rubí (p71)

La Vinya del Senyor (p71)

Getting There

Ⓜ **Metro** Jaume I station (line 4), on the southwestern side of La Ribera, is close to everything.

Ⓜ **Metro** Urquinaona (lines 1 and 4) is handy for the Palau de la Música Catalana, while Arc de Triomf (line 1) is good for Parc de la Ciutadella.

Top Sights
Museu Picasso

Pablo Picasso spent many years in Barcelona and, suitably, the city hosts the world's foremost museum dedicated to the artist's formative years and his extraordinary early talent; the cubist paintings for which he is best known are largely absent, but this is nonetheless a world-class gallery that traces his development as an artist. The building – five contiguous medieval stone mansions that span five centuries and yet have seamlessly become one – is itself a perfectly conceived work of art.

Map p64, D3

www.museupicasso.bcn.cat

Carrer de Montcada 15-23

adult/child €14/free, temporary exhibitions adult/child €6.50/free

⊙9am-7pm, to 9.30pm Thu

Ⓜ Jaume I

Museu Picasso

Don't Miss

The Child Artist

Rooms 1 & 2 The collection opens with sketches and oils from Picasso's earliest years in Málaga and La Coruña (around 1893–95), and lead on to his formative years in Barcelona. Some of his self-portraits and the portraits of his parents, which date from 1896, are evidence enough of his precocious talent. *Retrato de la Tía Pepa* (Portrait of Aunt Pepa), done in Málaga in 1896, shows the incredible maturity of his brushstrokes and his ability to portray character – at the tender age of 15.

Early Barcelona Days

Rooms 3 & 5 Picasso's early endeavours show a youthful talent searching for his style. In Room 3, his *Ciència i Caritat* (Science & Charity; painted in 1897 at age 16) is proof that, had he wanted, Picasso would have made a fine conventional artist. In Room 5, his studies of the styles of Velázquez and El Greco are fascinating insights into an artist perfecting his craft.

The Catalan Avant-Garde

Room 4 After a period spent in Horta de Sant Joan, he came back to Barcelona and joined what was known as the 'Catalan avant garde'. The work *Poeta Decadente* (Decadent Poet) is a portrait of his new friend Jaume Sabartés, who would remain one of Picasso's lifelong confidants – and later be the all-but-official curator of Picasso's works.

The Blue Period

Room 8 Before cubism took him across unexplored creative frontiers, Picasso went through

☑ Top Tips

▶ Understand this gallery for what it is: a fascinating insight into Picasso's early work with scarcely a cubist masterpiece in sight.

▶ Buy tickets online to avoid the long queues.

▶ Entry is free after 3pm Sunday and on the first Sunday of the month.

▶ Consider buying ArticketBCN (see the boxed text, p50) for combined admission to this and five other museums for €30.

✗ Take a Break

On Picasso's last visit to the city in 1934, El Xampanyet (p63) had already been open five years; it's still great for tapas.

Traditional Spanish tapas with subtle creative twists are the order of the day at young-at-heart Bar del Pla (p63), a little further northwest along Carrer de Montcada.

Museu Picasso

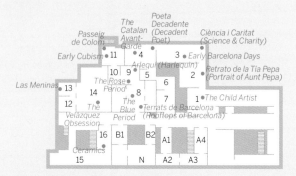

his first thematic adventure – the Blue Period. Lasting from 1901 to 1904, it coincided with his last years spent living in Barcelona. His nocturnal blue-tinted views of *Terrats de Barcelona* (Rooftops of Barcelona) are cold and cheerless, and yet somehow spectrally alive.

The Rose Period
Room 9 After the muted colours of the Blue Period, Picasso's palette fills with warm hues of pinks and oranges during his Rose Period, which unfolded in 1905. Harlequins, circus performers and acrobats make their appearance in his work. Although

painted toward the end of this period, *Arlequí* (Harlequin) is characteristic of the vibrant paintings from this time.

Early Cubism
Room 11 Picasso's masterworks lie elsewhere, but by 1917 his style was hinting at the cubist forms to come. During a six-month stay in Barcelona in 1917, he painted *Passeig de Colom* and *Blanquita Suárez,* which bear strong evidence of what was to follow. Another fine work here is the *Glass and Tobacco Packet* still-life painting, a simple and beautiful work.

The Velázquez Obsession

Rooms 12–14 The extent to which Picasso was influenced by the great masters is evident in these rooms, which contain an extraordinary 58-painting study of Diego Velázquez' masterpiece *Las Meninas* (which hangs in the Museo del Prado in Madrid). Painted in Cannes in 1957, these will satisfy your longing for Picasso's signature cubist style.

Ceramics

Room 15 What is also special about the Museu Picasso is its showcasing of his work in lesser-known mediums. The last rooms contain engravings and some 40 ceramic pieces completed throughout the latter years of his unceasingly creative life. You'll see plates and bowls decorated with simple, single-line drawings of fish, owls and other animal shapes, typical for Picasso's daubing on clay.

Understand

History of the Museum

Allegedly it was Picasso himself who proposed the museum's creation, to his friend and personal secretary, Jaume Sabartés, a Barcelona native, in 1960. Three years later, the 'Sabartés Collection' was opened, as a museum bearing Picasso's name would have been met with censorship – Picasso's opposition to the Franco regime was well known. The Museu Picasso we see today opened in 1983, and gradually expanded with donations from Salvador Dalí and Sebastià Junyer Vidal, among others, though most artworks were bequeathed by Picasso himself. His widow, Jacqueline Roque, also donated 41 ceramic pieces and the *Woman With Bonnet* painting after Picasso's death.

Top Sights
Basílica de Santa Maria del Mar

Nothing prepares you for the singular beauty of Basílica de Santa Maria del Mar. Barcelona's most stirring Gothic structure, the church stands serenely amid the crowds and clutter of buildings in El Born. In contrast to the tight warren of neighbouring streets, a real sense of light and space pervades the entire sanctuary of the church. Its interior is close to perfection wrought in stone, making this a worthy rival to La Catedral and La Sagrada Família for the affections of visitors to the city.

Map p64, D4

Plaça de Santa Maria del Mar

admission free

⊗ 9am-1.30pm & 4.30-8.30pm, opens at 10.30am Sun

Ⓜ Jaume I

Basílica de Santa Maria del Mar

Don't Miss

Main Sanctuary

The pleasing unity of form and symmetry of the church's central nave and two flanking aisles owed much to the rapidity with which the church was built in the 14th century – a mere 59 years, which must be a record for a major European house of worship. The slender, octagonal pillars create an enormous sense of lateral space bathed in the light of stained glass.

Ceiling & Side Chapels

Even before anarchists gutted the church in 1909 and again in 1936, Santa Maria always lacked superfluous decoration. Gone are the gilded chapels that weigh heavily over so many Spanish churches, while the splashes of colour high above the nave are subtle – unusually and beautifully so. It all serves to highlight the church's fine proportions, purity of line and sense of space.

The Porters

Look closely at the stones throughout the main sanctuary. One day a week during construction, the city's *bastaixos* (porters) carried these stones on their backs from the royal quarry in Montjuïc to the construction site. The memory of them lives on in reliefs in the main doors and stone carvings in the church, a reminder that this was conceived as a people's church.

El Fossar de les Moreres

Opposite the church's southern flank, an eternal flame burns high over a sunken square. This was El Fossar de les Moreres (the Mulberry Cemetery), where Catalan resistance fighters were buried after the siege of Barcelona ended in defeat in September 1714 during the War of the Spanish Succession.

☑ **Top Tips**

▶ If your purpose is spiritual, try to be here for the daily mass at 7.30pm.

▶ In summer you can visit the roof terrace as part of a guided tour (€5).

▶ Ask in the gift shop in case evening baroque music recitals are scheduled.

✗ **Take a Break**

Sit out the lunchtime hours when the church is closed at one of the outdoor tables at Bubó (p63), where tapas are accompanied by fine views of the western facade.

While you're waiting for the church to reopen, head upstairs for one of two balcony tables and choose from around 350 wines at La Vinya del Senyor (p71).

Local Life
Tapas & Bar Hopping in El Born

If there's one place that distils Barcelona's enduring cool to its essence and provides a snapshot of all that's irresistible about this city, it has to be El Born, the tangle of streets surrounding the Basílica de Santa Maria del Mar. Its secret is simple: this is where locals go for an authentic Barcelona night out.

1 Passeig del Born

Most nights, and indeed most things, in El Born begin along the Passeig del Born, one of the prettiest little boulevards in Europe. It's a place to sit as much as to promenade. In this graceful setting beneath the trees El Born's essential charms are obvious – thronging people, brilliant bars, and architecture that springs from a medieval film set.

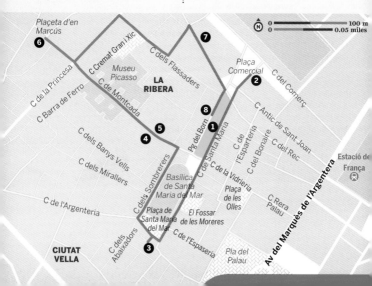

❷ Al Fresco Snacking

One of Barcelona's culinary delights, **Casa Delfín** (📞93 319 50 88; www.tallerdetapas.com; Passeig del Born 36; mains €10-15; ⏱8am-midnight daily, until 1am Fri & Sat; Ⓜ Barceloneta) is everything you dream of when you think of Catalan (and Mediterranean) cooking. Try some salt-strewn padron peppers, mussels, and Catalan coca flatbread. Grab a table on the square, with handsome views of the brick-and-iron **Born Centre Cultural**.

❸ Tapas with a View

Back in the heart of El Born, in the shadow of Basílica de Santa Maria del Mar, pastry chef Carles Mampel operates **Bubó** (📞93 268 72 24; www.bubo.es; Carrer de les Caputxes 6 & 10; tapas from €5; ⏱10am-9pm Mon-Thu & Sun, 10am-midnight Fri & Sat; Ⓜ Barceloneta). You'll find delectable desserts, snacks and an excellent sangria, best enjoyed at one of the outdoor tables facing the church.

❹ Catalan Tapas

Push through the crowd, order a *cava* (sparkling wine) and an assortment of tapas at **El Xampanyet** (📞93 319 70 03; Carrer de Montcada 22; ⏱noon-3.30pm & 7-11pm Tue-Sat, noon-4pm Sun; Ⓜ Jaume I), one of the city's best-known *cava* bars. Star dishes include tangy *boquerons en vinagre* (white anchovies in vinegar), and there's high-quality seafood served from a can in the Catalan way.

❺ Best of Basque

Having tasted Barcelona-style tapas, it's now time to compare it with the *pintxos* (Basque tapas of food morsels perched atop pieces of bread) lined up along the bar at **Euskal Etxea** (📞93 343 54 10; Placeta de Montcada 1; tapas from €2; ⏱10am-12.30am daily, until 1am Fri & Sat; Ⓜ Jaume I), a real slice of San Sebastián.

❻ Spain with a Twist

This detour to the northern limits of El Born is worth the walk. At first glance, the tapas at informal **Bar del Pla** (📞93 268 30 03; www.bardelpla. cat; Carrer de Montcada 2; mains from €10; ⏱noon-11pm Tue-Sun, until midnight Fri & Sat; Ⓜ Jaume I) are traditionally Spanish, but the riffs on a theme show an assured touch. Try the ham and roasted-meat croquettes or the marinated salmon, yoghurt and mustard.

❼ Tapas & Vermouth Pep

On the pedestrian Carrer del Rec, **Bormuth** (📞93 310 21 86; Carrer del Rec 31; tapas from €3.50; ⏱5pm-midnight Mon & Tue, noon-1am Wed, Thu & Sun, noon-2.30am Fri & Sat; Ⓜ Jaume I) serves all the old favourites – *patatas bravas, tortilla* – along with some less predictable and superbly prepared numbers (try the chargrilled red pepper with black pudding). Wash it down with a refreshing housemade vermouth.

❽ Buzzing Drinking Den

A spacious tavern in a Gothic building, **Miramelindo** (📞93 310 37 27; Passeig del Born 15; ⏱8pm-2.30am; Ⓜ Jaume I) remains a classic on Passeig del Born for mixed drinks. Try for a comfy seat at a table near the back before it fills to bursting.

A **B** **C** **D**

1

C de Trafalgar

Ptge de Sert

C de Trafalgar

12

C d'Ortigosa

C d'en Mònec

C de Sant Pere més Alt

C d'en Llàstics

C del Portal Nou

9

C del Comerç

Plaça
de Sant
Agustí Vell

2

Palau de
la Música
Catalana
1

C de Verdaguer
i Callís

C del Palau
de la Música

C de Sant Pere més Mitjà

C de Sant Pere més Baix

C dels Metges

C de Jaume Giralt

C d'en
Tantarantana

C d'Allada Vermell

Museu
de la
Xocolata
5

C del Fonollar

8

Plaça
d'Allada
i Vermell

C dels Carders

3

Via Laietana

C del Dr Joaquim Pou

LA RIBERA

Av de Francesc Cambó

C d'en Giralt i Pellisser

22

3

11

Mercat
de Santa
Caterina

C de les
Freixures

C dels
Mercaders

Plaça
d'Antoni
Maura

Plaça de Ramon
Berenguer
el Gran

C de Colomines

C dels Corders

C dels Assaonadors

C dels

Museu Europeu
d'Art Modern 6

C de Montcada

Museu
Picasso

C dels

4

Av de la Catedral

Plaça
Nova

C de Santa Llúcia

Plaça de
la Seu

Plaça de
Sant Iu

C de la Tapineria

Plaça
del Rei

C dels Comtes

BARRI
GÒTIC

C del Bisbe

C de la Llibreteria

C de Jaume I

Plaça de
l'Àngel

Jaume I

C de la Bòria

21

C de la Princesa

C dels Vigatans

C de l'Argenteria

Via Laietana

C dels Banys Vells

15

C dels
Mirallers

Basílica de
Santa Maria
del Mar

20

23

14

C de Manresa

C del Sotstinent Navarro

C de la Bassa

C de la Nau

C dels
Canvis Nous

C dels
Aguilers

25

Plaça de
Sant Just

Oficina d'Informació
de Turisme de Barcelona

CIUTAT
VELLA

5

For reviews see	
⊙ Top Sights	p56
⊙ Sights	p66
✕ Eating	p69
⦿ Drinking	p71
★ Entertainment	p71
⊟ Shopping	p72

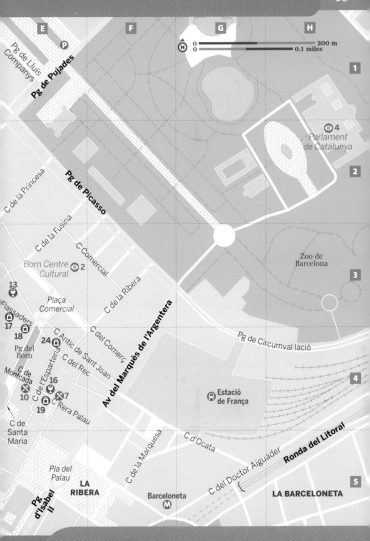

E

Pg de Lluís Companys

P

Pg de Pujades

F

G

0   200 m
N 0   0.1 miles

H

1

4
Parlament de Catalunya

2

Pg de Picasso

C de la Princesa

C de la Fusina

C Comercial

Born Centre Cultural 2

13

Plaça Comercial

C de la Ribera

Zoo de Barcelona

3

Flassaders

17

18

Pg del Born

24

C Antic de Sant Joan

C del Comerç

C de l'Esparteria

C del Rec

16

Av del Marquès de l'Argentera

Pg de Circumval·lació

10

C de Montcada

7

19

C Rera Palau

Estació de França

4

C de Santa Maria

Pla del Palau

C de la Marquesa

C d'Ocata

C del Doctor Aiguader

Ronda del Litoral

LA BARCELONETA

5

Pg d'Isabel II

LA RIBERA

Barceloneta M

LA BARCELONETA

Local Life

A Walk in the Park

The handsomely landscaped **Parc de la Ciutadella** (Map p48, G2; Passeig de Picasso; admission free; MArc de Triomf) is a local favourite for a leisurely promenade. The park is the site of Catalonia's regional parliament, the city zoo, some eye-catching buildings and the monumental *Cascada* (waterfall) created between 1875 and 1881 by Josep Fontsère with the help of a young Antoni Gaudí.

Sights

Palau de la Música Catalana

ARCHITECTURE

1 Map p64, A2

This concert hall is a high point of Barcelona's Modernista architecture, a symphony in tile, brick, sculpted stone and stained glass. Built by Domènech i Montaner between 1905 and 1908 for the Orfeo Català musical society, it was conceived as a temple for the Catalan Renaixença (Renaissance). (☑93 295 72 00; www.palaumusica.org; Carrer de Sant Francesc de Paula 2; adult/child €17/free; ☺guided tours 10am-3.30pm daily; MUrquinaona)

Born Centre Cultural

HISTORIC BUILDING

2 Map p64, E3

Launched to great fanfare in 2013 as part of the events held for the tercentenary of the Catalan defeat in the War of the Spanish Succession, this cultural space is housed in the former Mercat del Born, a handsome 19th-century structure of slatted iron and brick. Excavation in 2001 unearthed remains of whole streets flattened to make way for the much-hated citadel *(ciutadella)* – these are now on show on the exposed subterranean level. (☑93 256 68 51; www.elborncentrecultural.bcn.cat; Plaça Comercial 12; centre free, exhibition spaces adult/child €6/free; ☺10am-8pm Tue-Sun; MBarceloneta)

Mercat de Santa Caterina

MARKET

3 Map p64, C3

Come shopping for your tomatoes at this extraordinary-looking produce market, designed by Enric Miralles and Benedetta Tagliabue to replace its 19th-century predecessor. Finished in 2005, it is distinguished by its kaleidoscopic and undulating roof, held up above the bustling produce stands, restaurants, cafes and bars by twisting slender branches of what look like grey steel trees. (☑93 319 17 40; www.mercatsantacaterina.com; Avinguda de Francesc Cambó 16; ☺7.30am-2pm Mon, to 3.30pm Tue, Wed & Sat, to 8.30pm Thu & Fri, closed afternoons Jul & Aug; ☜; MJaume I)

Parlament de Catalunya

NOTABLE BUILDING

4 Map p64, H2

Southeast, in the fort's former arsenal, is the regional Parlament de Catalunya. You can join free guided tours, in Catalan and Spanish (Castilian) only, on

Palau de la Música Catalana

Saturdays and Sundays. The building is open for independent visiting on 11 September from 10am to 7pm. The most interesting is the sweeping Escala d'Honor (Stairway of Honour) and the several solemn halls that lead to the Saló de Sessions, the semicircular auditorium where parliament sits. At the centre of the garden in front of the *parlament* is a statue of a seemingly heartbroken woman, *Desconsol* (Distress; 1907), by Josep Llimona. (www.parlament.cat; ☷guided tours 10am-1pm Sat, Sun & holidays)

Museu de la Xocolata   MUSEUM

5 ◉ Map p64, D2

Chocoholics have a hard time containing themselves in this museum dedicated to the fundamental foodstuff – particularly when faced with tempting displays of cocoa-based treats in the cafe at the exit. (☏93 268 78 78; www.museuxocolata.cat; Carrer del Comerç 36; adult/senior & student/child under 7yr €5/4.25/free; ☷10am-7pm Mon-Sat, to 3pm Sun & holidays; ☷☷; ⓜJaume I)

Museu Europeu d'Art Modern   MUSEUM

6 ◉ Map p64, D3

The European Museum of Modern Art opened in the summer of 2011 in the Palau Gomis, a handsome 18th-century mansion around the corner from the Museu Picasso. The art within is strictly representational (the

Understand
Catalan Gothic

- -

The Historical Context
The emergence of the soaring Gothic style of architecture in France in the 13th century coincided with an expanding Catalan empire, the rise of a trading class and a burgeoning mercantile sphere of influence. The enormous cost of building the grand new monuments could thus be covered by the steady increase in Barcelona's wealth.

The architectural style reflected developing building techniques. The introduction of flying buttresses and ribbed vaulting in ceilings allowed engineers to raise edifices loftier and seemingly lighter than ever before. The pointed arch became standard and great rose windows offered a way to bring light inside these enormous spaces.

Catalan Difference
Catalan Gothic rarely followed the same course as the style in northern Europe. Decorations are more sparing; another distinctive characteristic is the triumph of breadth over height. While northern European cathedrals reach for the sky, Catalan Gothic structures push to the sides, stretching the vaulting design to the limit.

The Saló del Tinell in the Museu d'Història de Barcelona, with a parade of 15m arches (among the largest ever built without reinforcement) holding up the roof, is a perfect example of Catalan Gothic. Another is the present home of the Museu Marítim, Barcelona's medieval shipyards. In churches too, the Catalans opted for robust shape and lateral space – step into the Basílica de Santa Maria del Mar and you'll soon get the idea.

Also a notable departure from northern Gothic styles is the lack of spires and pinnacles. Bell towers tend to terminate in a flat or nearly flat roof. Occasional exceptions prove the rule. The main facade of Barcelona's Catedral, with its three gnarled and knobbly spires, does vaguely resemble the outline that confronts you in the cathedrals of Chartres or Cologne. But then this was a 19th-century addition, admittedly constructed to an existing medieval design.

Most of Barcelona's Gothic heritage lies within the boundaries of the old city but a few examples can be found beyond, notably the Museu-Monestir de Pedralbes in Sarrià.

'Modern' of the name simply means 'contemporary') and is mostly from young Spanish artists, though there are some works from elsewhere in Europe. (MEAM; www.meam.es; Carrer Barra de Ferro 5; adult/concession/child €7/5/free; ⏱10am-8pm Tue-Sun; Ⓜ Jaume I)

Eating

Cal Pep   TAPAS $$

7 Map p64, E4

It's getting a foot in the door here that's the problem – there can be queues out into the square with people trying to get in. And if you want one of the five tables out the back, you'll need to call ahead. Most people are happy elbowing their way to the bar for some of the tastiest gourmet seafood tapas in town. (☎93 310 79 61; www.calpep.com; Plaça de les Olles 8; mains €12-20; ⏱7.30-11.30pm Mon, 1-3.45pm & 7.30-11.30pm Tue-Fri, 1-3.45pm Sat, closed last 3 weeks Aug; Ⓜ Barceloneta)

El Atril   INTERNATIONAL $$

8 Map p64, C2

Aussie owner Brenden is influenced by culinary influences from all over the globe, so while you'll see plenty of tapas (the *patatas bravas* are recommended for their homemade sauce), you'll also find kangaroo fillet, salmon and date rolls with mascarpone, chargrilled turkey with fried yucca, and plenty more. If the weather is good

or there's no room in the cosy dining room, there are tables outside in a lively square. (☎93 310 12 20; www.atril barcelona.com; Carrer dels Carders 23; mains €11-15; ⏱6pm-midnight Mon, noon-midnight Tue-Thu, noon-1am Fri & Sat, 11.30am-11.30pm Sun; Ⓜ Jaume I)

Comerç 24   INTERNATIONAL $$$

9 Map p64, D1

Michelin-starred chef Carles Abellán playfully reinterprets the traditional (suckling pig 'Hanoi style'), as well as more international classics, such as the bite-sized mini-pizza sashimi with tuna, *melón con jamón,* a *millefeuille* of layered caramelised Iberian ham and thinly sliced melon, or oxtail with cauliflower purée. If your budget will stretch to it, try a little of almost

---

Local Life

Fish for People in the Know

There's no sign, but locals know where to head for a feast. The raw ingredients at **Passadís del Pep** (Map p48, E5; ☎93 310 10 21; www.passadis.com; Pla del Palau 2; mains €18-23; ⏱1.15-3.45pm Mon-Sat; Ⓜ Barceloneta) are delivered from fishing ports along the Catalan coast. There's no menu – what's on offer depends on what the sea has surrendered that day. Just head down the ill-lit corridor and entrust yourself to the restaurant's care.

everything with the 'Menú del Gran Festival' (€116). (📞93 319 21 02; www.carlesabellan.com; Carrer del Comerç 24; mains €24-32; ⏱1.30-3.30pm & 8.30-11pm Tue-Sat; Ⓜ Barceloneta)

La Llavor dels Orígens
CATALAN $

10 Map p64, E4

In this treasure chest of Catalan regional products, the shop shelves groan under the weight of bottles and packets of goodies. It also has a long menu of smallish dishes, such as *sopa de carbassa i castanyes* (pumpkin and chestnut soup) or *mandonguilles amb albergínies* (rissoles with aubergine), that you can mix and match over wine by the glass. (📞93 310 75 31; www.lallavordelsorigens.com; Carrer de la Vidrieria 6-8; mains €8-11; ⏱12.30pm-midnight; Ⓜ Jaume I)

Local Life
A Blissful Spa

With low lighting and relaxing perfumes wafting around you, **Aire De Barcelona** (Map p"Map:10-la-ribera-pk-bar4" on page 64, E2; 📞93 295 57 43; www.airedebarcelona.com; Passeig de Picasso 22; thermal baths & aromatherapy €29; ⏱10am-10pm Mon-Wed & Sun, 10am-2am Thu-Sat; Ⓜ Arc de Triomf) could be the perfect way to end a day. Hot, warm and cold baths, steam baths and options for various massages, including on a slab of hot marble, make for a delicious hour or so. Book ahead and bring a swimming costume.

Cuines de Santa Caterina
MEDITERRANEAN, ASIAN $$

11 Map p64, B3

With a contemporary feel and open kitchens, this multifaceted eatery inside the Mercat de Santa Caterina offers all sorts of food. Peck at the sushi bar, tuck into classic rice dishes or go vegetarian. It does some things better than others, so skip the hummus and *tarte Tatin*. A drawback is the speed with which barely finished plates are whisked away from you, but the range of dishes and bustling atmosphere are fun. Reservations aren't taken, so it's first come first served. (📞93 268 99 18; www.grupotragaluz.com; Mercat de Santa Caterina; mains €10-14; ⏱1-4pm & 8pm-midnight daily, until 1am Fri & Sat; Ⓜ Jaume I)

En Aparté
FRENCH $

12 Map p64, C1

A great low-key place to eat good-quality French food, just off the quiet Plaça de Sant Pere. The restaurant is small but spacious, with sewing-machine tables and vintage details, and floor-to-ceiling windows that bring in some wonderful early-afternoon sunlight. (📞93 269 13 35; www.enaparte.es; Carrer Lluis el Piados 2; mains €7-10; ⏱10am-1am Tue-Thu, 10am-2am Fri & Sat, noon-1am Sun; 📶; Ⓜ Arc de Triomf or Urquinaona)

Drinking

Juanra Falces
COCKTAIL BAR

13 Map p64, E3

Transport yourself to a Humphrey Bogart movie in this narrow little bar, formerly (and still, at least among the locals) known as Gimlet. White-jacketed bar staff with all the appropriate aplomb will whip you up a gimlet or any other classic cocktail (around €10) your heart desires. (☎93 310 10 27; Carrer del Rec 24; ⊙8pm-3am, from 10pm Mon & Sun; MJaume I)

La Vinya del Senyor
WINE BAR

14 Map p64, D5

Relax on the *terrassa,* which lies in the shadow of Basílica de Santa Maria del Mar, or crowd inside at the tiny bar. The wine list is as long as *War and Peace* and there's a table upstairs for those who opt to sample by the bottle rather than the glass. (☎93 310 33 79; www.lavinyadelsenyor.com; Plaça de Santa Maria del Mar 5; ⊙noon-1am Mon-Thu, noon-2am Fri & Sat, noon-midnight Sun; MJaume I)

Rubí
BAR

15 Map p64, D4

With its boudoir lighting and cheap mojitos, Rubí is where the Born's cognoscenti head for a nightcap – or several. It's a narrow, cosy space – push through to the back where you might just get one of the coveted tables – with superior bar food, from Vietnamese rolls to more traditional selections of cheese and ham. (☎647 773707; Carrer dels Banys Vells 6; ⊙7.30pm-2.30am; MJaume I)

Mudanzas
BAR

16 Map p64, E4

This was one of the first bars to get things into gear in El Born and it still attracts a faithful crowd. It's a straightforward place for a beer, a chat and perhaps a sandwich. Oh, and it has a nice line in rums and malt whiskey. (☎93 319 11 37; Carrer de la Vidrieria 15; ⊙9.30am-2.30am Mon-Fri, 5pm-3am Sat & Sun; ☎; MJaume I)

Entertainment

Palau de la Música Catalana
CLASSICAL MUSIC

A feast for the eyes, this Modernista confection is also the city's most traditional venue for classical and choral music (see 1 Map p64, A2), although it has a wide-ranging program, including flamenco, pop and – particularly – jazz. Just being here for a performance is an experience. Sip a preconcert tipple in the foyer, its tiled pillars all a-glitter. Head up the grand stairway to the main auditorium, a whirlpool of Modernista whimsy. (☎93 295 72 00; www.palaumusica.org; Carrer de Sant Francesc de Paula 2; ⊙box office 9.30am-9pm Mon-Sat; MUrquinaona)

Shopping

Loisaida
CLOTHING, ANTIQUES

17 Map p64, E3

A sight in its own right, housed in what was once the coach house and stables for the Royal Mint, Loisaida (from the Spanglish for 'Lower East Side') is a deceptively large emporium of colourful, retro and somewhat preppy clothing for men and women, costume jewellery, music from the 1940s and '50s and some covetable antiques. There is more womenswear and some very cute children's lines a few doors away at **No 32** (✆93 295 54 92; Carrer dels Flassaders 32; ⏱11am-9pm Mon-Sat, 11am-2pm & 4-8pm Sun; Ⓜ Jaume I). (✆93 295 54 92; www.loisaidabcn.com; Carrer dels flassaders 42; ⏱11am-9pm Mon-Sat, 11am-2pm & 4-8pm Sun; Ⓜ Jaume I)

Hofmann Pastisseria
FOOD

18 Map p64, E4

With old timber cabinets, this bite-sized gourmet patisserie, linked to the prestigious Hofmann cooking school, has an air of timelessness. Choose between jars of delicious chocolates, the day's croissants and more dangerous pastries, or an array of cakes and other sweets. (✆93 268 82 21; www.hofmann-bcn.com; Carrer dels flassaders 44; ⏱9am-2pm & 3.30-8pm Mon-Thu, 9am-8.30pm Fri & Sat, 9am-2.30pm Sun; Ⓜ Jaume I)

Custo Barcelona
FASHION

19 Map p64, E4

The psychedelic decor and casual atmosphere lend this avant-garde Barcelona fashion store a youthful edge. Custo presents daring new women's and men's collections each year on the New York catwalks. The dazzling colours and cut of anything from dinner jackets to hot pants are for the uninhibited. It has five other stores around town. (✆93 268 78 93; www.custo-barcelona.com; Plaça de les Olles 7; ⏱10am-9pm Mon-Sat, noon-8pm Sun; Ⓜ Jaume I)

Casa Gispert
FOOD

20 Map p64, D4

The wonderful, atmospheric and wood-fronted Casa Gispert has been toasting nuts and selling all manner of dried fruit since 1851. Pots and jars piled high on the shelves contain an unending variety of crunchy titbits: some roasted, some honeyed, all of them moreish. Your order is shouted over to the till, along with the price, in a display of old-world accounting. (✆93 319 75 35; www.casagispert.com; Carrer dels Sombrerers 23; ⏱9.30am-2pm & 4-8.30pm Tue-Fri, 10am-2pm & 5-8.30pm Sat; Ⓜ Jaume I)

Arlequí Màscares
ARTS & CRAFTS

21 Map p64, C4

A wonderful little oasis of originality, this shop specialises in masks for costume and decoration. Some of the pieces are superb, while stock also includes a beautiful range of decorative boxes in Catalan themes, and some old-style marionettes. (✆93 268 27 52; www.arlequimask.com; Carrer de la Princesa 7; ⏱10.30am-8.30pm Mon-Sat, 10.30am-3pm & 4-7.30pm Sun; Ⓜ Jaume I)

Olisoliva   FOOD

 22 Map p64, B3

Inside the Mercat de Santa Caterina,
this simple, glassed-in store is stacked
with olive oils and vinegars from all
over Spain. Taste some of the products
before deciding. Some of the best olive
oils come from southern Spain. The
range of vinegars is astounding too.
(☑93 268 14 72; www.olisoliva.com; Mercat
de Santa Caterina; ☺9.30am-3pm Mon-Wed &
Sat, 9.30am-8pm Fri, Sat; Ⓜ Jaume I)

El Magnífico   COFFEE

 23 Map p64, D4

All sorts of coffee has been roasted
here since the early 20th century. The
variety of coffee (and tea) available
is remarkable – and the aromas hit
you as you walk in. Across the road,
the same people run the exquisite
and much newer tea shop **Sans i
Sans** (☑93 310 25 18; Carrer de l'Argenteria
59; Ⓜ Jaume I). (☑93 319 39 75; www.
cafesmagnifico.com; Carrer de l'Argenteria
64; ☺10am-8pm Mon-Sat; Ⓜ Jaume I)

Coquette   FASHION

 24 Map p64, E4

With its spare, cut-back and designer
look, this fashion store is attractive
in its own right. Women can browse
through casual, feminine wear by
such designers as Humanoid, Vanessa
Bruno, UKE, Hoss Intropia and others,
with a further collection nearby at
Carrer de Bonaire 5. (☑93 295 42 85;

Wine and olive tasting

www.coquettebcn.com; Carrer del Rec 65;
☺11am-3pm & 5-9pm Mon-Fri, 11.30am-9pm
Sat; Ⓜ Barceloneta)

Vila Viniteca   DRINK

25 Map p64, D5

One of the best wine stores in Barcelona (and Lord knows, there are a
few), this place has been searching out
the best in local and imported wines
since 1932. At No 9 it has another store
devoted to gourmet food products.
(☑902 32 77 77; www.vilaviniteca.es; Carrer
dels Agullers 7; ☺8.30am-8.30pm Mon-Sat;
Ⓜ Jaume I)

Explore

Barceloneta & the Beaches

Barcelona's waterfront is a fascinating corner of the city – a place where avant-garde public art is juxtaposed with the gritty thorough-fares of La Barceloneta, an 18th-century fisherfolk's district. It's in the restaurants of the latter that you'll find the city's best seafood and rice dishes, while beaches stretch away to the north.

The Sights in a Day

Begin with a journey through Catalan history at the **Museu d'Història de Catalunya** (p80), take a return trip aboard the **Transbordador Aeri** (p80) for fine waterfront views, then head for **L'Aquàrium** (p80), one of Spain's best aquariums.

Most afternoons in La Barceloneta revolve around food and beaches. For the former, we suggest tapas at **Jai-Ca** (p82) or **Vaso de Oro** (p77), but leave room for a sit-down meal at **Can Majó** (p82). The perfect response to such gastronomic excess is to lie down, and this is best done at any beach that takes your fancy from La Barceloneta to Port Olímpic and beyond.

There are loads of great settings for a drink in the area. Festive **Can Paixano** (p76) has ever-flowing glasses of *cava*, while **Absenta** (p84) and **Ké?** (p84) draw a more bohemian crowd. For Mediterranean views, opt for **Santa Marta** (p85) or one of the summertime **chiringuitos** (p85), where you can sip cocktails while digging your heels in the sand. Near Port Olímpic is another row of waterfront bars, which adopt more of a nightclub vibe as the evening progresses.

For a local's day by the beach, see p76.

 Local Life

Sea & Seafood (p76)

 Best of Barcelona

Seafood Restaurants
Barraca (p82)

Can Maño (p82)

Jai-Ca (p82)

Can Majó (p82)

Drinking Spots
Absenta (p84)

Can Paixano (p76)

Vaso de Oro (p77)

Santa Marta (p85)

Chiringuitos (p85)

Getting There

M Metro Drassanes (line 3) is best for the southwestern end of the port, Barceloneta (line 4) for La Barceloneta, and Ciutadella Vila Olímpica (line 4) for the beaches and Port Olímpic.

🚌 Bus Numbers 17, 39 and 64 all converge on La Barceloneta.

Cable Car If you're coming from Montjuïc, the Transbordador Aeri (cable car) is best.

Local Life
Sea & Seafood

Barcelona's Mediterranean roots are nowhere more pronounced than in La Barceloneta, a seaside peninsula with a salty air and an enduring relationship with the sea. As often as not, this is one area where locals outnumber tourists, at least on weekends when the city's restaurants and beaches throng with a predominantly local crowd.

1 The Cava Crowd

Welcome to Barcelona as it once was. It doesn't come any more authentic than **Can Paixano** (☑93 310 08 39; Carrer de la Reina Cristina 7; tapas €3-6; ⏱9am-10.30pm Mon-Sat; Ⓜ Barceloneta), one of the best old-style *cava* (sparkling wine) bars in Barcelona. This ageless bar serves up the pink stuff in elegant little glasses, provided you can elbow your way through the crowds to order.

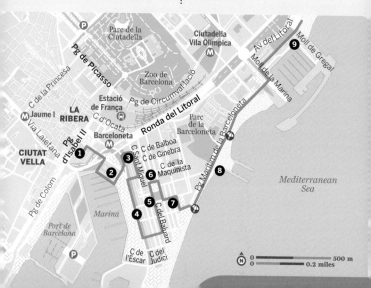

2 Seaside Views

Head up to the top floor of the **Museu d'Història de Catalunya** (you don't need to buy a ticket) to the elegant seafood restaurant **1881** (✆93 221 00 50; www.sagardi.com; Plaça de Pau Vila 3; mains €14-28; ◷10am-midnight Tue-Sun; 🛜; Ⓜ Barceloneta). Step out onto the terrace for a lovely view over the marina.

3 Beer & Prawns

If you like noisy, crowded bars, high-speed staff ready with a smile, a cornucopia of tapas and the illusion, in here at least, that Barcelona hasn't changed in decades, come to **Vaso de Oro** (Carrer de Balboa 6; tapas €4-12; ◷10am-midnight; Ⓜ Barceloneta). This place brews its own beers and the tapas are delicious (try the grilled prawns).

4 A Waterfront Stroll

Maybe it's a good thing the Metro doesn't reach the beach at La Barceloneta, obliging you to walk down the sunny portside promenade of **Passeig de Joan de Borbó**. Megayachts sway gently on your right as you bowl down a street crackling with activity.

5 Mouth-watering Tapas

There's no sign and the setting is decidedly downmarket, but tiny **Cova Fumada** (✆93 221 40 61; Carrer del Baluard 56; tapas €3.50-7.50; ◷9am-3.20pm Mon-Wed, 9am-3.20pm & 6-8.20pm Thu & Fri, 9am-1.20pm Sat; Ⓜ Barceloneta) always packs in a crowd. The secret? Mouthwatering small plates cooked to perfection in the small open kitchen.

6 Market Buzz

Set in a modern glass and steel building in the heart of the neighbourhood, **Mercat de la Barceloneta** (✆93 221 64 71; www.mercatdelabarceloneta.com; Plaça de la Font 1; ◷7am-3pm Mon-Thu & Sat, 7am-8pm Fri; Ⓜ Barceloneta) has the usual array of fresh veg and seafood stalls, as well as places to enjoy a sit-down meal. Across the street, don't miss **Baluard Barceloneta**, one of the city's best bakeries.

7 Iconic Drinking Den

Bar Leo (Carrer de Sant Carles 34; ◷noon-9.30pm; Ⓜ Barceloneta) is a hole-in-the-wall drinking spot plastered with images of late Andalucian singer and heart-throb Bambino, and a jukebox mostly dedicated to flamenco. For a youthful, almost entirely *barcelonin* crowd, Bar Leo is it!

8 Barcelona's Beaches

There are prettier beaches elsewhere on earth, but none so handy for the world's coolest city. **Platja de Sant Sebastià**, closest to Barceloneta, yields to **Platja de la Barceloneta**, and both are broad and agreeably long sweeps of sand.

9 An Olympic Port

A 1.25km promenade shadows the waterfront all the way to the restaurant-lined marina of **Port Olímpic** (Ⓜ Ciutadella Vila Olímpica). An eye-catcher on the approach from La Barceloneta is Frank Gehry's giant copper *Peix* (Fish) sculpture, while just to the north is the enticing **Platja de Nova Icària**.

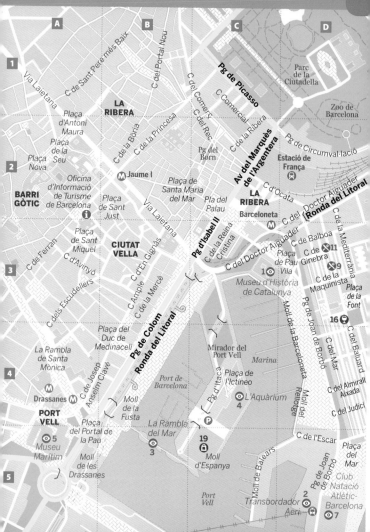

E

C de Wellington
Universitat Pompeu Fabra
Parc de Carles I

M
Ciutadella Vila Olímpica

Pg de Circumval·lació

Ronda del Litoral
Av del Litoral

C de Trelawny

F

C de Moscou

C de Salvador Espriu
Plaça dels Voluntaris
Av del Litoral

C de Ramon Trias Fargas

C de la Marina

Moll de Mestral

G

Port Olímpic

14
Moll de Gregal

H

1

😀17

2

Platja de la Barceloneta

Pg Marítim de la Barceloneta

Parc de la Barceloneta

Pg de Salvat Papasseit

🪧

3

C d'Andrea Dòria
LA BARCELONETA

13
15 C de Sant Carles
C de Ginebra
12 ❌8
🪧
C de l'Almirall Cervera

❌18
10
Platja de Sant Sebastià

Mediterranean Sea

4

◎6
Boardriders Barceloneta

Platja de Sant Miquel

🧭 N
0 — 400 m
0 — 0.2 miles

For reviews see
◎ Sights	p80
❌ Eating	p82
😀 Drinking	p84
🛍 Shopping	p85

5

Sights

Museu d'Història de Catalunya   MUSEUM

1 ⊙ Map p78, C3

Inside the **Palau de Mar**, this worthwhile museum covers the Stone Age through to the early 1980s. It is a busy hotchpotch of dioramas, artefacts, models, documents and interactive bits: all up, an entertaining exploration of 2000 years of Catalan history. (Museum of Catalonian History; ☑ 93 225 47 00; www.mhcat.net; Plaça de Pau Vila 3; adult/child €4.50/3.50, 1st Sun of month free; ⊙ 10am-7pm Tue & Thu-Sat, to 8pm Wed, to 2.30pm Sun; M Barceloneta)

Transbordador Aeri   CABLE CAR

2 ⊙ Map p78, D5

This cable car strung across the harbour to Montjuïc provides an eagle-eye view of the city. The cabins float between the Torre de Sant Sebastià (in La Barceloneta) and Miramar (Montjuïc), with a midway stop at the Torre de Jaume I in front of the World Trade Center. At the top of the Torre de Sant Sebastià is a restaurant, **Torre d'Alta Mar** (☑ 93 221 00 07; www.torredealtamar. com; Torre de Sant Sebastià, Passeig de Joan Borbó 88; mains around €35; ⊙ 1-3.30pm Tue-Sat & 8-11.30pm daily; ☐ 17, 39, 57 or 64, M Barceloneta). (www.telefericodebarcelona.com; Passeig Escullera; one way/return €11/16.50; ⊙ 11am-7pm; ☐ 17, 39 or 64, M Barceloneta)

La Rambla del Mar   WATERFRONT

3 ⊙ Map p78, B5

The city's authorities extended the world-famous La Rambla thoroughfare out into the sea in the early 2000s, connecting the city with the reclaimed port area of Port Vell. Seeming to float above the water, it offers reasonable views of the waterfront.

L'Aquàrium   AQUARIUM

4 ⊙ Map p78, C4

It is hard not to shudder at the sight of a shark gliding above you, displaying its toothy grin. But the 80m shark tunnel is the highlight of one of Europe's largest aquariums. It has the world's best Mediterranean collection and plenty of colourful fish from as far off as the Red Sea, the Caribbean and the Great Barrier Reef. All up, some 11,000 fish of 450 species reside here. (☑ 93 221 74 74; www.aquariumbcn.com; Moll d'Espanya; adult/child €20/15, dive €300; ⊙ 9.30am-11pm Jul & Aug, to 9pm Sep-Jun; M Drassanes)

Local Life

Beachfront Art

American Rebecca Horn's striking sculptural tribute to La Barceloneta, **Homenatge a la Barceloneta** is an eye-catching column of rusted-iron-and-glass cubes on Platja de Sant Sebastià. Erected in 1992, it pays homage to the beach bars and restaurants that disappeared around the time of the Olympic Games, and hence it has earned the respect of even the crustiest local old-timers.

L'Aquàrium

Museu Marítim

MUSEUM

5 Map p78, A5

Gothic shipyards, a relic from Barcelona's days as the seat of a seafaring empire, house the Museu Marítim, which includes a full-sized replica of Don Juan of Austria's 16th-century flagship, fishing vessels and antique navigation charts. (☎93 342 99 20; www.mmb.cat; Avinguda de les Drassanes; adult/child €5/2, 3-8pm Sun free; ☺10am-8pm; ☂; Ⓜ Drassanes)

Boardriders Barceloneta

WATER SPORTS

6 Map p78, E5

Facing the seafront, Boardriders rents out surfboards (per hour/half-day €12/25), stand-up paddleboards (per hour/half-day €15/30) and wetsuits. It also sells clothes and gear. (☎93 221 44 91; Carrer de la Drassana 10; ☺10am-8pm Mon-Sat, from 11am Sun; Ⓜ Barceloneta)

Club Natació Atlètic-Barcelona

SWIMMING

7 Map p78, D5

This athletic club has one indoor and two outdoor pools. Of the latter, one is heated for lap swimming in winter. Admission includes use of the gym and private beach access. (www.cnab.cat; Plaça del Mar; daypass adult/child €12.20/7.10; ☺7am-11pm Mon-Sat, 8am-8pm Sun; 🚌17, 39, 57 or 64, Ⓜ Barceloneta)

Local Life

Antique Market

At the base of La Rambla, the small **Port Antic Market** (Map p78, A5; Plaça del Portal de la Pau; ⊙10am-8pm Sat & Sun; Ⓜ Drassanes) is a requisite stop for strollers and antique hunters. Find old photographs, frames, oil paintings, records, cameras, vintage toys and other odds and ends.

Eating

Barraca   SEAFOOD $$$

 8 Map p78, E4

Recently opened, this buzzing space has a great location fronting the Mediterranean – a key reference point in the excellent seafood dishes served up here. Start off with a cauldron of chili-infused clams, cockles and mussels before moving on to the lavish paellas and other rice dishes, which steal the show. (☑ 93 224 12 53; www.barraca-barcelona.com; Passeig Maritim de la Barceloneta 1; mains €19-29; ⊙1pm-midnight; Ⓜ Barceloneta)

Can Maño   SPANISH $

 9 Map p78, D3

It may look like a dive, but you'll need to be prepared to wait for a seat for a night of *raciones* (full-plate-size tapas serving; posted on a board at the back) over a bottle of *turbio* (a cloudy white plonk). The first-rate seafood is abundant. (Carrer del Baluard 12; mains €7-12; ⊙9am-4pm Tue-Sat & 8-11pm Mon-Fri; Ⓜ Barceloneta)

Can Majó   SEAFOOD $$$

10   Map p78, E4

Virtually on the beach (with tables outside in summer), Can Majó has a long and steady reputation for fine seafood, particularly its rice dishes and bountiful *suquets* (fish stews). Sit outside (there are heat lamps in winter) and admire the beach goers. (☑ 93 221 54 55; www.canmajo.es; Carrer del Almirall Aixada 23; mains €16-26; ⊙1-4pm Tue-Sun & 8-11.30pm Tue-Sat; ☐ 45, 57, 59, 64 or 157, Ⓜ Barceloneta)

Jai-Ca   SEAFOOD $

11   Map p78, D3

Jai-Ca is a much-loved eatery that serves up juicy grilled prawns, flavour-rich anchovies, tender octopus, decadent razor clams and other seafood favourites to ever-growing crowds as the evening progresses. The turbio (Galician white wine), sangria and cold draughts are ideal refreshment after a day on the beach. (☑ 93 268 32 65; Carrer de Ginebra 13; tapas €4-7; ⊙9am-11.30pm Mon-Sat; Ⓜ Barceloneta)

Maians   TAPAS $

12 Map p78, E4

This tiny jovial bar and eatery in Maians serves excellent tapas to a hip, largely neighbourhood crowd. Highlights include the *cazón en adobo* (marinated fried dogfish) and *mejillones a la marinera* (mussels in a rich tomato broth) followed by hearty *arroz negra* (paella with cuttlefish). (☑ 93 221 10 20; Carrer de Sant Carles 28; tapas €4-7; ⊙1-4pm & 8-11pm Tue-Sat; Ⓜ Barceloneta)

Understand

The Changing Fortunes of Catalonia

Catalan identity is a multifaceted phenomenon, but Catalans are, more than anything else, united by the collective triumphs and shared grievances of the region's tumultuous past.

The Catalan golden age began in the early 12th century when Ramon Berenguer III, who already controlled Catalonia and parts of southern France, launched the region's first seagoing fleet. In 1137 his successor, Ramon Berenguer IV, was betrothed to the one-year-old heiress to the Aragonese throne, thereby giving Catalonia sufficient power to expand its empire out into the Mediterranean. By the end of the 13th century, Catalan rule extended to the Balearic Islands and Catalonia's seaborne trade brought fabulous riches.

But storm clouds were gathering; weakened by a decline in trade and foreign battles, Catalonia was vulnerable. And when Fernando became king of Aragón in 1479 and married Isabel, Queen of Castile, Catalonia became a province of Castile. Catalonia resented its new subordinate status but could do little to overturn it. After backing the losing side in the War of Spanish Succession (1702–13), Barcelona rose up against the Spanish crown whose armies besieged the city from March 1713 until 11 September 1714. The victorious Felipe V abolished Catalan self-rule, built a huge fort (the Ciutadella) to watch over the city, banned writing and teaching in the Catalan language, and farmed out Catalonia's colonies to other European powers.

Trade again flourished from Barcelona in the following centuries, and by the late 19th and early 20th centuries there were growing calls for greater self-governance to go with the city's burgeoning economic power. However, after Spanish general Francisco Franco's victory in 1939, Catalan Francoists and the dictator's army shot in purges at least 35,000 people, most of whom were either anti-Franco or presumed to be so. Over time, the use of Catalan in public was banned, all street and town names were changed into Spanish, and Castellano Spanish was the only permitted language in schools and the media. Franco's lieutenants remained in control of the city until his death in 1975 and the sense of grievance in Barcelona remains, more than three decades after self-government was restored in Catalonia in 1977. You'll see this reflected in the near-universal use of Catalan in public, the prevalence of Catalan flags and a general revival in Catalan culture.

Top Tip

Seaside Spin

Stretching over 4km from Barceloneta to Parc del Fòrum, the beachside bike path makes a breezy setting for a spin. Open-air cafes and restaurants are ideal pitstops along the way. Loads of places hire bikes, including **BarcelonaBiking.com** (☑ 656 356300; www.barcelonabiking.com; Baixada de Sant Miquel 6; bike hire per hr/24hr €5/15, tour €21; ⊙10am-8pm, tour 11am daily; ⓂJaume I or Liceu) in Barri Gòtic and **My Beautiful Parking** (☑93 186 73 65; www.mybeautiful-parking.com; Carrer Viagatans 2; bike hire per 2hr/24hr €6/15; ⊙10am-9pm Mon-Sat; ⓂJaume I or Liceu) in La Ribera.

El Ben Plantat   INTERNATIONAL $

13 Map p78, E3

A welcome addition to seafood-centric Barceloneta, El Ben Plantat serves a varied menu of small plates, with excellent vegetarian choices (humus, guacamole and chips, tofu pâté, vegie burgers). On weekdays you'll also find multicourse lunch specials – mussels with potatoes, homemade falafel, veal stew, vegetable croquettes – good value at €8. (☑93 624 38 32; Carrer de Sant Carles 21; tapas €4-11; ⊙9am-5pm Mon-Wed, to 11.45pm Thu-Fri, 11am-11.45pm Sat, to 7pm Sun; ☑; ⓂBarceloneta)

El Cangrejo Loco   SEAFOOD $$$

14 Map p78, G1

Of the hive of eating activity along the docks of Port Olímpic, the 'Mad Crab' is among the best. Fish such as sea bass and monkfish are served in various guises and melt in the mouth. For utter decadence, there's a seafood platter, which has lobster, prawns, razor clams, crayfish and other delights. (☑93 221 05 33; www.elcangrejoloco.com; Moll de Gregal 29-30; mains €15-28, menú del día €26; ⊙1-4pm & 8pm-midnight; ⓂCiutadella Vila Olímpica)

Drinking

Absenta   BAR

15 Map p78, E3

Decorated with old paintings, vintage lamps and curious sculpture (including a dangling butterfly woman and face-painted TVs), this whimsical and creative drinking den takes its liquor seriously. Stop in for the house-made vermouth or for more bite try one of the many absinthes on hand. Absenta gathers a hipsterish but easygoing crowd. (Carrer de Sant Carles 36; ⊙7pm-2am Wed-Thu, from 1pm Sat & Sun; ⓂBarceloneta)

Ké?   BAR

16 Map p78, D3

An eclectic and happy crowd hangs about this small bohemian bar run by a friendly Dutchman. Pull up a padded 'keg chair' or grab a seat on one of the worn lounges at the back and join in the animated conversation wafting out over the street. Outdoor seating in summer, just a few steps from Barceloneta's market. (Carrer del Baluard 54; ⊙noon-2am; ⓂBarceloneta)

CDLC

LOUNGE

17 Map p78, F2

Seize the night by the scruff at the Carpe Diem Lounge Club, where you can lounge in Asian-inspired surrounds. Ideal for a slow warm-up before heading to the nearby clubs. You can come for the food or wait until about midnight, when the DJs and dancers take full control. (www.cdlcbarcelona.com; Passeig Marítim de la Barceloneta 32; noon-4am; M Ciutadella Vila Olímpica)

Santa Marta

BAR

18 Map p78, E4

This chilled bar just back from the beach attracts a garrulous mix of locals and expats, who come for light meals, beers and prime people-watching at one of the outdoor tables near the boardwalk. It has some tempting food too: a mix of local and Italian items, with a range of satisfying sandwiches. (Carrer de Guitert 60; 9.30am-midnight; 45, 57, 59 or 157, M Barceloneta)

Shopping

Maremàgnum

MALL

19 Map p78, C5

Created out of largely abandoned docks, this buzzing shopping centre, with bars, restaurants and cinemas, is pleasant enough for a stroll virtually in the middle of the old harbour. The usual labels are on hand, including Spanish chain Mango, mega-retailer

Preparing desserts at a *chiringuito* (open-air bar)

H&M and Barcelona-based Desigual. Football fans will be drawn to FC Botiga. (www.maremagnum.es; Moll d'Espanya 5; 10am-10pm; M Drassanes)

Local Life

Beach Bars

From late April to October, *chiringuitos* (open-air bars) arrive on the beach, bringing a tropical air to the city with music, cocktails and a laid-back vibe. These are also great snack spots, offering sandwiches, ice cream and tapas plates; some even have a full menu. You can't beat the setting: refuelling while watching the waves lapping on the shore.

Explore

Passeig de Gràcia & L'Eixample

L'Eixample, bisected by the monumental Passeig de Gràcia, is the sophisticated alter ego to Barcelona's old city. This is where Modernisme left its most enduring mark and it's here that some of the city's most iconic architectural landmarks reside. With elegant shops, terrific restaurants and pulsating nightlife, it all adds up to one of the city's most rewarding neighbourhoods.

The Sights in a Day

☀ The earlier you get to **Casa Batlló** (p90) and **La Pedrera** (p104) the better your chances of avoiding a queue. If you linger over the weird-and-wonderful detail of these sites, you could easily spend a couple of hours in each, which should just leave time to admire **Casa Amatller** (p96) and get the lowdown on contemporary art at the **Fundació Antoni Tàpies** (p96).

☀ Take a break from museums with a tapas crawl that takes in the full range of tapas traditions at **Tapas 24** (p99), **Taktika Berri** (p99) and **Cata 1.81** (p99), followed by some shopping at **Vinçon** (p92), **Joan Múrria** (p104) and **Camper** (p104), among others. Finish off the afternoon at the **Museu del Modernisme Català** (p97).

☾ L'Eixample nights can be long and liquid, but we suggest one last Modernista fling: dinner at **Casa Calvet** (p101), with its otherwise-inaccessible Gaudí interiors. **Les Gens Que J'Aime** (p103) is a great place to ease into the evening, while **Dry Martini** (p103) is another favourite. End the night at upscale club **Astoria** (p104), or with a touch of live salsa at **Antilla BCN** (p103).

For a local's day of shopping in L'Eixample, see p92.

◉ Top Sights

La Pedrera (p104)

Casa Batlló (p90)

◷ Local Life

Shop in the Quadrat d'Or (p92)

♥ Best of Barcelona

Tapas
Cata 1.81 (p99)

Tapas 24 (p99)

Modernista Buildings
La Pedrera (p104)

Casa Batlló (p90)

Fundació Antoni Tàpies (p96)

Casa Amatller (p96)

Palau del Baró Quadras (p98)

Getting There

Ⓜ **Metro** Passeig de Gràcia (lines 2, 3 and 4) and Diagonal (lines 3, 5 and 7) are in the heart of L'Eixample.

Ⓜ **Metro** Around L'Eixample's perimeter are Catalunya, Universitat, Hospital Clínic, Verdaguer and Girona.

FGC Provença and Passeig de Gràcia stations.

Top Sights
La Pedrera

One of the Passeig de Gràcia's, and indeed Barcelona's, most beautiful Modernista structures, La Pedrera – officially called Casa Milà after its owners, but nicknamed La Pedrera (The Stone Quarry) by bemused locals who watched Gaudí build it from 1905 to 1910 – is in the top tier of Gaudí's achievements. Conceived as an apartment block, its approach to space and to light and its blurring of the dividing line between decoration and functionality will leave you gasping at the sheer originality of it all.

Map p94, D2

Carrer de Provença 261-265

adult/student/child €16.50/14.85/8.25

🕙9am-8pm Mar-Oct, to 6.30pm Nov-Feb

Ⓜ Diagonal

Interior courtyard, La Pedrera

Don't Miss

The Facade

The natural world was one of the most enduring influences on Gaudí's work, and La Pedrera's undulating grey stone facade evokes a cliff-face sculpted by waves and wind. The wave effect is emphasised by elaborate wrought-iron balconies that bring to mind seaweed washed up on the shore. The lasting impression is of a building on the verge of motion.

The Roof Terrace

Gaudí's blend of mischievous form with ingenious functionality is evident on the roof, with its clusters of chimneys, stairwells and ventilation towers that rise and fall atop the structure's wave-like contours like giant medieval knights. Some are unadorned, others are decorated with *trencadís* (ceramic fragments) and even broken *cava* bottles. The deep patios, which Gaudí treated like interior facades, flood the apartments with natural light.

Espai Gaudí

With 270 gracious parabolic arches, the Espai Gaudí (Gaudí Space) feels like the fossilised ribcage of some giant prehistoric beast. At one point, 12 arches come together to form a palm tree. Watch out also for the strange optical effect of the mirror and hanging sculpture on the east side.

La Pedrera Apartment

Below the attic, the apartment (El Pis de la Pedrera) spreads out. Bathed in evenly distributed light, twisting and turning with the building's rippling distribution, the labyrinthine apartment is Gaudí's vision of domestic bliss. In the ultimate nod to flexible living, the apartment has no load-bearing walls: the interior walls could thus be moved to suit the inhabitants' needs.

☑ Top Tips

▶ It's well worth the extra €4 for the audio guide (there's even a children's version).

▶ La Pedrera is extremely popular: buy tickets online and arrive at opening time to avoid the worst of the crowds.

▶ Guided evening tours show the mysterious side of La Pedrera. Reserve a spot in advance.

▶ On Thursday to Saturday, from mid-June to early September, La Pedrera hosts open-air concerts on the roof.

✕ Take a Break

One block west of La Pedrera, La Bodegueta Provença (p102) is a classy spot serving first-rate tapas and wines by the glass.

An excellent anytime choice (coffee and croissants, or tapas for lunch or dinner), Cerveseria Catalana (p101) lies two blocks south near the Rambla de Catalunya.

Top Sights
Casa Batlló

If La Sagrada Família is Gaudí's master symphony, Casa Batlló is his whimsical waltz – not to mention one of the weirdest-looking concoctions to emerge from his fantastical imagination. From the playful genius of its facade to its revolutionary experiments in light and architectural form (straight lines are few and far between), Casa Batlló, which was built as an anything-but-humble apartment block, is one of the most beautiful buildings in this city where competition for such a title is fierce.

Map p94, E3

www.casabatllo.es

Passeig de Gràcia 43

adult/concessions/
child under 7yr
€21.50 / €18.50/free

🕙9am-9pm daily

Ⓜ Passeig de Gràcia

Casa Batlló

Don't Miss

The Facade

To Salvador Dalí it resembled 'twilight clouds in water'. Others see a more-than-passing resemblance to the Impressionist masterpiece *Water Lilies* by Claude Monet. A Rorschach blot for our imagination, Casa Batlló's facade is exquisite and fantastical, sprinkled with fragments of blue, mauve and green tiles, and studded with wave-shaped window frames and mask-like balconies.

Sala Principal

The staircase wafts you to the 1st floor, where everything swirls in the main salon: the ceiling twists into a whirlpool-like vortex around its sun-like lamp; the doors, window and skylights are dreamy waves of wood and coloured glass in mollusc-like shapes. The sense of light and space here is extraordinary thanks to the wall-length window onto Passeig de Gràcia.

Back Terrace

Opening onto an expansive L'Eixample patio, Casa Batlló's back terrace is like a fantasy garden in miniature. It's a place where flowerpots take on strange forms and where the accumulation of *trencadís* (broken ceramic pieces) – a mere 330 of them on the building's rear facade – has the effect of immersing you in a kaleidoscope.

The Roof

Casa Batlló's roof, with the twisting chimney pots so characteristic of Gaudí's structures, is the building's grand crescendo. The eastern end represents Sant Jordi (St George) and the Dragon; one local name for Casa Batlló is the *casa del drac* (house of the dragon). The ceaseless curves of coloured tiles have the effect of making the building seem like a living being.

☑ Top Tips

▶ Queues to get in are frequent, so buy tickets online and go early in the morning.

▶ Although Casa Batlló stays open until 9pm, the last entry tickets are sold at 8pm.

▶ Even if you've already visited, return after sunset to see the facade illuminated in all its glory.

✗ Take a Break

Two short blocks down the hill and just off the other side of Passeig de Gràcia, Tapas 24 (p99) is one of Barcelona's most innovative tapas bars.

A short walk west of Casa Batlló, Alba Granados (p102) is a typical modern L'Eixample restaurant, offering great cooking and wines in a relaxed setting.

Local Life
Shop in the Quadrat d'Or

While visitors to L'Eixample do the sights, locals go shopping in the Quadrat d'Or, the grid of streets either side of the Passeig de Gràcia. This is Barcelona at its most fashion- and design-conscious, which also describes a large proportion of L'Eixample's residents. All the big names are here, alongside boutiques of local designers who capture the essence of Barcelona cool.

....

❶ Designer Barcelona
It has a reputation as the essence of innovative Catalan design and the frame in which Spanish design evolves, but **Vinçon** (☎93 215 60 50; www.vincon.com; Passeig de Gràcia 96; ◷10am-8.30pm Mon-Fri, 10.30am-9pm Sat; ⓜDiagonal) has its roots in L'Eixample. Pamper your aesthetic senses with a journey through its household wares.

❷ The New Wave

Detour for a moment off Passeig de Gràcia to **Lurdes Bergada** (📞 93 218 48 51; www.lurdesbergada.es; Rambla de Catalunya 112; 🕙 10.30am-8.30pm Mon-Sat; Ⓜ Diagonal), a boutique run by mother-and-son designer team Lurdes Bergada and Syngman Cucala. The classy men's and women's fashions use natural fibres and have attracted a cult following.

❸ A Pastry Stop

Time for a break. Few pastry shops have such a long-established pedigree as **Mauri** (📞 93 215 10 20; www.pastelerias mauri.com; Rambla de Catalunya 102; pastries from €3.40; 🕙 8am-midnight Mon-Sat, 9am-4pm Sun; Ⓜ Diagonal): the plush interior is capped by an ornate fresco dating back to Mauri's first days in 1929. Its croissants and feather-light *ensaïma-das* (sweet buns) are near perfect.

❹ Modernista Jewellery

This is more than just any old jewellery store. The boys from **Bagués-Masriera** (📞 93 216 01 74; www.masriera.es; Passeig de Gràcia 41; 🕙 10am-8.30pm Mon-Fri, 11am-8pm Sat; Ⓜ Passeig de Gràcia) have been moulding metal since the 19th century, and many of the classic pieces here have a flighty, Modernista influence. Service can seem haughty, but owes much to old-school courtesies.

❺ Father of Fashion

While bags and suitcases in every conceivable colour of buttersoft leather are the mainstay at **Loewe** (📞 93 216 04 00; www.loewe.com; Passeig de Gràcia 35; 🕙 10am-8.30pm Mon-Sat; Ⓜ Passeig de Gràcia), there is also a range of clothing for men and women, along with some stunning – and stunningly priced – accessories. The shop itself is worth a visit, beautifully housed in the **Casa Lleó Morera**.

❻ Say It With Chocolate

A sleek and modern temple to the sweet stuff, **Cacao Sampaka** (📞 93 272 08 33; www.cacaosampaka.com; Carrer del Consell de Cent 292; 🕙 9am-9pm Mon-Sat; Ⓜ Passeig de Gràcia) doubles as a shop and café. Select from every conceivable flavour (rosemary, perhaps?) and fill your own elegant little gift box.

❼ Fine Wines

For superior souvenirs in liquid form, head to the state-of-the-art **Monvínic** (📞 932 72 61 87; www.monvinic.com; Carrer de la Diputació 249; 🕙 wine bar 1.30-11pm Mon-Sat; Ⓜ Passeig de Gracia), a veritable palace of wine with some 3,000 options in its cellar, including some extremely rare finds. Try before you buy in the chic and snappy wine bar.

❽ Chill Down

Cosmo (www.galeriacosmo.com; Carrer d'Enric Granados 3; 🕙 10am-10pm Mon-Thu, 10am-midnight Fri & Sat, 11am-10pm Sun; Ⓜ Universitat) is a bright cavernous space, dotted with colour from the exhibitions that adorn its high white walls. It has a nice selection of teas, cakes and snacks, and, set on a pleasant pedestrian strip, it's perfect for an evening tipple outside or in.

A **B** **C** **D**

C d'Alfons XII

Travessera de Gràcia

C d'Aribau

C de Tuset

C de Mola

Plaça de Narcis Oller

Via Augusta

C de Sèneca

C de Bonavista

C de Còrsega

Plaça de Joan Carles I

Palau del Baró Quadras **7**

C de Pau Claris

1

Diagonal **M**

Fundació Suñol **8**

La Pedrera

Av Diagonal

C de Balmes

Diagonal **M**

Pg de Gràcia

24

C d'Enric Granados

C de Rosselló

17

Rambla de Catalunya

28

2

20

Provença **M**

26

L'ESQUERRA DE L'EIXAMPLE

14

C de Londres

C de Paris

C de Còrsega

19

C d'Aribau

C de Mallorca

16

Fundació Antoni Tàpies **1**

C de Casanova

C de Villarroel

22

Plaça del Doctor Ferrer Cajigal

C de Muntaner

C d'Aragó

C d'Enric Granados

3

Plaça del Doctor Letamendi

Museu del Modernisme Català **6**

C de Provença

11

13

10

M Hospital Clínic

C de Casanova

4

C del Rosselló

C del Comte d'Urgell

C de València

Universitat de Barcelona

Plaça de la Universitat

23

Av de Roma

C d'Aragó

C de la Diputació

C de Casanova

5

C del Comte Borrell

C del Consell de Cent

C de Villarroel

C de Sepúlveda

Gran Via de les Corts Catalanes

Ronda de Sant Antoni

18

Urgell **M**

For reviews see

💿	Top Sights	p88
💿	Sights	p96
✖	Eating	p98
🍷	Drinking	p103
🛍	Shopping	p104

E Verdaguer

Av Diagonal

F

G

H

C de Sicília

9

Casa de les Punxes

L'EIXAMPLE

C de Mallorca

C de Girona

C de Bailèn

C de Nàpols

C de Roger de Flor

Pg de Sant Joan

Gran Vía de les Corts Catalanes

1

4 Palau Montaner

C de València

C de Roger de Llúria

C d'Aragó

C del Bruc

C del Consell de Cent

25

M Girona

Plaça de Tetuan

M Tetuan

Pg de Sant Joan

2

21

C del Bruc

C de la Diputació

Passeig de Gràcia

M

C de Pau Claris

C de Casp

C d'Ausiàs Marc

C d'Alí Bei

Casa Batlló

Casa Amatller

3

2

29

12

30

Pg de Gràcia

Casa Lleó Morera

15

Arc de Triomf M

3

Ronda de Sant Pere

C de Trafalgar

Plaça de Sant Pere

Plaça de Joan Carles I

5

Jardins de la Reina Victòria

Plaça d'Urquinaona

M Urquinaona

Fundación Francisco Godia

Rambla de Catalunya

27

Urquinaona

C d'Ortigosa

C de Sant Pere més Alt

C de Sant Pere més Baix

4

Catalunya

M

Oficina d'Informació de Turisme de Barcelona

Via Laietana

Plaça de Catalunya

LA RIBERA

M Universitat

C de Pelai

C de Bergara

Catalunya

C de Santa Anna

Av del Portal de l'Àngel

C Comtal

Plaça d'Antoni Maura

C dels Tallers

C de la Canuda

Plaça Nova

Plaça de la Seu

Jaume I M

5

C de Valldonzella

Plaça de Vicenç Martorell

La Rambla

BARRI GÒTIC

Plaça de Joan Coromines

EL RAVAL

N

0   400 m
0   0.2 miles

Sights

Fundació Antoni Tàpies GALLERY

1 ⊙ Map p94, D3

The Fundació Antoni Tàpies is both a pioneering Modernista building (completed in 1885) and the major collection of leading 20th-century Catalan artist Antoni Tàpies. Known for his esoteric work, Tàpies died in February 2012, aged 88; he leaves behind a powerful range of paintings and a foundation intended to promote contemporary artists. (📞93 487 03 15; www.fundaciotapies.org; Carrer d'Aragó 255; adult/concession €7/5.60; ⊙10am-7pm Tue-Sun; Ⓜ Passeig de Gràcia)

Top Tip

Modernisme Unpacked

Aficionados of Barcelona's Modernista heritage should consider the **Ruta del Modernisme pack** (www.rutadelmodernisme.com). For €12 you receive a guide to 115 Modernista buildings great and small, a map, and discounts of up to 50% on the main Modernista sights in Barcelona, as well as some in other municipalities around Catalonia. For €18 you get another guide and map, *Sortim*, which leads you to bars and restaurants located in Modernista buildings. Pick up the packs at the main tourist office at Plaça de Catalunya 17-S or the Pavellons Güell (open 10am to 2pm Saturday and Sunday) in Pedralbes.

Casa Lleó Morera ARCHITECTURE

2 ⊙ Map p94, E3

Domènech i Montaner's 1905 contribution to the Manzana de la Discordia, with Modernista carving outside and a bright, tiled lobby in which floral motifs predominate, is perhaps the least odd-looking of the three main buildings on the block. In 2014 part of the building was opened to the public (by guided tour only), so you can appreciate the rich mosaics and whimsical decor. (📞93 676 27 33; www.casalleomorera.com; Passeig de Gràcia 35; adult/concession/child under 12yr €15/€13.50/free; ⊙guided tour in English 10am Mon-Sat; Ⓜ Passeig de Gràcia)

Casa Amatller ARCHITECTURE

3 ⊙ Map p94, E3

One of Puig i Cadafalch's most striking bits of Modernista fantasy, Casa Amatller combines Gothic window frames with a stepped gable borrowed from Dutch urban architecture. But the reliefs of dragons, knights and other characters dripping off the main facade are pure caprice. Renovations will see the 1st (main) floor converted into a museum, while the 2nd floor will house the Institut Amatller d'Art Hispanic (Amatller Institute of Hispanic Art). (📞93 487 72 17; www.amatller.org; Passeig de Gràcia 41; tour €10; ⊙tour Sat; Ⓜ Passeig de Gràcia)

Palau Montaner ARCHITECTURE

4 ⊙ Map p94, E2

Interesting on the outside and made all the more enticing by its gardens, this

Facades of Casa Amatller and Casa Batlló

creation by Domènech i Montaner is spectacular on the inside. Completed in 1896, its central feature is a grand staircase beneath a broad, ornamental skylight. The interior is laden with sculptures (some by Eusebi Arnau), mosaics and fine woodwork. It is currently only open, by guided tour, to groups by prior arrangement. (☏93 317 76 52; www.rutadelmodernisme.com; Carrer de Mallorca 278; adult/child & senior €6/3; Ⓜ Passeig de Gràcia)

Fundación Francisco Godia
GALLERY

5 ◉ Map p94, E4

Francisco Godia (1921–90), head of one of Barcelona's great establishment families, liked fast cars (he came sixth in the 1956 Grand Prix season driving Maseratis) and fine art. An intriguing mix of medieval art, ceramics and modern paintings make up this varied private collection. (☏93 272 31 80; www.fundacionfgodia.org; Carrer de la Diputació 250; adult/student/child under 6yr €6/3/free; ☉10am-8pm Mon & Wed-Sat, 10am-3pm Sun; Ⓜ Passeig de Gràcia)

Museu del Modernisme Català
MUSEUM

6 ◉ Map p94, D4

Housed in a Modernista building, the ground floor seems like a big Modernista furniture showroom. Several items by Antoni Gaudí, including chairs from

Local Life
Carrer d'Enric Granados

Half the city's population would like to live on Carrer d'Enric Granados. The pedestrianised end, at Carrer de la Diputació, is marked off by the **Universitat de Barcelona gardens** (Map p94, D4; ☉10am-sunset Mon-Fri from Plaça de l'Universitat, 10am-sunset Sat & Sun from Carrer de la Diputació). The banter of diners can be heard at nearby restaurants as you wander rows of elegant apartments to the leafy Plaça del Doctor Letamendi. From here, one lane of traffic trickles along up to Avinguda Diagonal (this end is also pedestrian only).

Casa Batlló and a mirror from Casa Calvet, are supplemented by a host of items by his lesser-known contemporaries, including whimsical, mock medieval pieces by Puig i Cadafalch. (☎93 272 28 96; www.mmcat.cat; Carrer de Balmes 48; adult/concession €10/€8.50; ☉10am-8pm Mon-Sat, to 2pm Sun; ⓂPasseig de Gràcia)

Palau del Baró Quadras ARCHITECTURE

 7 Map p94, D1

Puig i Cadafalch designed Palau del Baró Quadras (built 1902–06) in an exuberant Gothic-inspired style. The main facade is its most intriguing, with a soaring, glassed-in gallery. Look closely at the gargoyles and reliefs – the sword-wielding knight and pair of toothy fish clearly have the same artistic signature as the architect behind Casa Amatller. Decor inside is dominated by Middle

Eastern and East Asian themes. (☎93 467 80 00; Avinguda Diagonal 373; admission free; ☉8am-8pm Mon-Fri; ⓂDiagonal)

Fundació Suñol GALLERY

 8 Map p94, D2

Rotating exhibitions of portions of this private collection of mostly 20th-century art (some 1200 works in total) offer anything from Man Ray's photography to sculptures by Alberto Giacometti. Over two floors, you are most likely to run into Spanish artists, anyone from Picasso to Jaume Plensa, along with a sprinkling of others from abroad. (☎93 496 10 32; www.fundacio sunol.org; Passeig de Gràcia 98; adult/concession/child €4/2/free; ☉11am-2pm & 4-8pm Mon-Fri, 4-8pm Sat; ⓂDiagonal)

Casa de les Punxes ARCHITECTURE

9 Map p94, E1

Puig i Cadafalch's Casa Terrades is better known as the Casa de les Punxes (House of Spikes) because of its pointed turrets. This apartment block, completed in 1905, looks like a fairytale castle and has the singular attribute of being the only fully detached building in L'Eixample. (Casa Terrades; Avinguda Diagonal 420; ⓂDiagonal)

Eating

Cinc Sentits INTERNATIONAL $$$

 10 Map p94, C4

Enter the realm of the 'Five Senses' to indulge in a jaw-dropping tasting

menu (there is no à la carte, although dishes can be tweaked to suit diners' requests), consisting of a series of small, experimental dishes. A key is the use of fresh local produce, such as fish landed on the Costa Brava and top-quality suckling pig from Extremadura, along with the kind of creative genius that has earned chef Jordi Artal a Michelin star. (☎93 323 94 90; www.cinc sentits.com; Carrer d'Aribau 58; tasting menus €65-109; ☺1.30-3pm & 8.30-10pm Tue-Sat; ⓜPasseig de Gràcia)

Cata 1.81 TAPAS $$

11 Map p94, C4

A beautifully designed venue (with lots of small lights, some trapped in bird-cages), this is the place to come for fine wines and dainty gourmet dishes like *raviolis amb bacallà* (salt-cod dumplings) or *truita de patates i tòfona negre* (thick potato tortilla with a delicate trace of black truffle). The best option is to choose from one of several tasting-menu options ranging from €29 to €45. (☎93 323 68 18; www.cata181.com; Carrer de València 181; tapas €6-8; ☺7pm-midnight Mon-Sat; ⓜPasseig de Gràcia)

Tapas 24 TAPAS $$

12 Map p94, E3

Carles Abellan, master of Comerç 24 in La Ribera, runs this basement tapas haven known for its gourmet versions of old faves. Specials include the *bikini* (toasted ham and cheese sandwich – here the ham is cured and the truffle makes all the difference)

and a thick black *arròs negre de sípia* (squid-ink black rice). (☎93 488 09 77; www.carlesabellan.com; Carrer de la Diputació 269; tapas €4-9; ☺9am-midnight Mon-Sat; ⓜPasseig de Gràcia)

Taktika Berri BASQUE, TAPAS $$

13 Map p94, C4

Get in early because the bar teems with punters from far and wide, anxious to wrap their mouths around some of the best Basque tapas in town. The hot morsels are all snapped up as soon as they arrive from the kitchen, so keep your eyes peeled. The seated dining area out the back is also good. In the evening, it's all over by about 10.30pm. (☎93 453 47 59; Carrer de València 169; tapas from €3; ☺1-4pm & 8.30-11pm Mon-Fri, 1-4pm Sat; ⓜHospital Clínic)

Local Life
Hidden Restaurant
True to name, **Speakeasy** (☎93 217 50 80; www.javierdelasmuelas.com; Carrer d'Aribau 162-166; mains €19-28; ☺1-4pm & 8pm-midnight Mon-Fri, 8pm-midnight Sat, closed Aug; ⓜDiagonal) is a clandestine restaurant lurking behind the Dry Martini (p103) bar. You will be shown a door through the open kitchen area to the 'storeroom', lined with hundreds of bottles of backlit, quality tipples. The menu has tempting options like the wild mushroom ravioli with langoustine or venison with puréed sweet potato.

Understand

Modernisme

In the late 19th century, Barcelona was booming and the city's culture of avant-garde experimentation was custom made for a group of outrageously talented architects who came to be known as Modernistas. Leading the way was Antoni Gaudí i Cornet (1852–1926). Gaudí personifies and largely transcends a movement that brought a thunderclap of innovative greatness to an otherwise middle-ranking European city.

Modernisme did not appear in isolation in Barcelona. To the British and French the style was art nouveau; the Germans called it Jugendstil (Youth Style). Whatever it was called, a key uniting element was the sensuous curve, implying movement, lightness and vitality. Modernista architects looked to the past for inspiration: Gothic, Islamic and Renaissance design in particular. At its most playful, Modernisme was able to intelligently flout the rule books of these styles and create exciting new cocktails.

The Architects

Gaudí and the two architects who most closely followed him in talent, Lluís Domènech i Montaner (1850–1923) and Josep Puig i Cadafalch (1867–1957), were Catalan nationalists. The political associations are significant, as Modernisme became a means of expression for Catalan identity; the style barely touched the rest of Spain.

Gaudí took great inspiration from Gothic styles, but he also sought to emulate the harmony he observed in nature. Straight lines were out. The forms of plants and stones were in. Gaudí used complex string models weighted with plumb lines to make his calculations. The architect's work is at once a sublime reaching-out to the heavens, and an earthy appeal to sinewy movement.

The Materials & Decoration

Stone, unclad brick, exposed iron and steel frames, and copious use of stained glass and ceramics in decoration, were all features of the new style. Modernista architects relied heavily on the skills of craftsmen who were the heirs of the guild masters and had absorbed centuries of know-how about working with these materials. There were no concrete pours. Gaudí in particular relied on the old skills and even ran schools in La Sagrada Família workshops in a bid to keep them alive. Newer materials, such as forged iron, also came into their own during this period.

Ceiling light, Casa Batlló (p90)

Cerveseria Catalana   TAPAS $

14 Map p94, D3

The 'Catalan Brewery' is good for breakfast, lunch and dinner. Come for your morning coffee and croissant, or wait until lunch to enjoy choosing from the abundance of tapas and *montaditos* (canapés). You can sit at the bar, on the pavement terrace or in the restaurant at the back. The variety of hot tapas, salads and other snacks draws a well-dressed crowd of locals and outsiders. (☏93 216 03 68; Carrer de Mallorca 236; tapas €4-11; ⊙9.30am-1.30am; Ⓜ Passeig de Gràcia)

Casa Calvet   CATALAN $$$

15 Map p94, G3

An early Gaudí masterpiece loaded with his trademark curvy features now houses a swish restaurant (just to the right of the building's main entrance). Dress up and ask for an intimate *taula cabina* (wooden booth). You could opt for sole and lobster on mashed leeks, with balsamic vinegar and Pedro Ximénez reduction, and artichoke chips. It has various tasting menus for up to €70, and a lunch menu for €34. (☏93 412 40 12; www. casacalvet.es; Carrer de Casp 48; mains €26-31; ⊙1-3.30pm & 8.30-11pm Mon-Sat; Ⓜ Urquinaona)

Alba Granados SPANISH, MEDITERRANEAN $$

16 Map p94, C3

In summer ask for one of the romantic tables for two on the 1st-floor balcony. Overlooking the trees, it is a unique spot, with little traffic. Inside, the ground- and 1st-floor dining areas are huge, featuring exposed brick and dark parquet. The menu offers a little of everything but the best dishes revolve around meat, such as *solomillo a la mantequilla de trufa con tarrina de patata y beicon* (sirloin in truffle butter, potato and bacon terrine). (📞93 454 61 16; www.albagranados.cat; Carrer d'Enric Granados 34; mains €14-28; ⏱1-4pm & 8pm-midnight; 🚉FGC Provença)

Local Life
Eco-Friendly Cafe

A project in sustainability all round, **Fastvínic** (Map p94, E4; 📞93 487 32 41; www.fastvinic.com; Carrer de la Diputació 251; sandwiches €4.25-12; ⏱noon-midnight Mon-Sat; Ⓜ Passeig de Gracia) is slow food done fast, with ingredients, wine and building materials all sourced from Catalonia. Designed by Alfons Tost, there are air-purifying plants, energy-efficient LED lighting, and a water and food recycling system. It's all sandwiches on the menu, with some wonderful choices like crunchy suckling pig, banana chutney and coriander.

La Bodegueta Provença TAPAS $$

17 Map p94, C2

The 'Little Wine Cellar' offers classic tapas presented with a touch of class, from *calamares a la andaluza* (lightly battered squid rings) to *cecina* (dried cured veal meat). The house speciality is *ous estrellats* (literally 'smashed eggs') – a mix of scrambled egg white, egg yolk, potato and then ingredients ranging from foie gras to *morcilla* (black pudding). Wash it all down with a good Ribera del Duero or *caña* (little glass) of beer. Staff can be a bit curt. (📞93 215 17 25; Carrer de Provença 233; mains €11-25; ⏱8am-4pm & 8-11.30pm; Ⓜ Diagonal)

Amaltea VEGETARIAN $

18 Map p94, C5

The ceiling fresco of blue sky sets the scene in this popular vegetarian eatery. The *menú del día* (€10.70) offers a series of dishes that change frequently with the seasons. At night, the set two-course dinner (€15) offers good value. The homemade desserts are tempting. The place is something of an alternative lifestyle centre, with yoga, t'ai chi and belly-dancing classes. (www.amalteaygovinda.com; Carrer de la Diputació 164; mains €5-9; ⏱1-4pm & 8-11.30pm Mon-Sat; 🖉; Ⓜ Urgell)

Cremeria Toscana GELATERIA $

19 Map p94, B3

Yes, you can stumble across quite reasonable ice cream in Barcelona, but close your eyes and imagine yourself across the Mediterranean with the real ice-cream wizards. Creamy *stracciatella* and wavy *nocciola* and myriad other flavours await at the most authentic gelato outlet in town. Buy a cone or a tub. (☑93 539 38 25; www.cremeria-toscana.es; Carrer de Muntaner 161; ice cream from €2.80; ⏱1pm-midnight Tue-Sun; Ⓜ Hospital Clínic)

Drinking

Dry Martini
BAR

20 Map p94, B2

Waiters with a discreetly knowing smile will attend to your cocktail needs here. The house drink, taken at the bar or in one of the plush green leather lounges, is a safe bet. The gin and tonic comes in an enormous mug-sized glass – a couple of these and you're well on the way. Out the back is a restaurant, **Speakeasy**. (☑93 217 50 72; www.javierdelasmuelas.com; Carrer d'Aribau 162-166; ⏱1pm-2.30am Mon-Thu, 6pm-3am Fri & Sat; Ⓜ Diagonal)

Les Gens Que J'Aime
BAR

21 Map p94, E2

This intimate basement relic of the 1960s follows a deceptively simple formula: chilled jazz music in the background, minimal lighting from an assortment of flea-market lamps and a cosy, cramped scattering of red velvet-backed lounges around tiny dark tables. (☑93 215 68 79; www.lesgensquejaime.com; Carrer de València 286; ⏱6pm-2.30am Sun-Thu, 7pm-3am Fri & Sat; Ⓜ Passeig de Gràcia)

Top Tip
The Gaixample
The area just above Gran Via de les Corts Catalanes and to the left of Rambla de Catalunya is popularly known as the 'Gaixample', for its proliferation of gay bars and restaurants. For listings, see p173.

La Fira
BAR

22 Map p94, B3

A designer bar with a difference. Wander in past distorting mirrors and ancient fairground attractions from Germany. Put in coins and listen to hens squawk. Speaking of squawking, the music swings wildly from whiffs of house through '90s hits to Spanish pop classics. You can spend the earlier part of the night trying some of the bar's shots – it claims to have 500 varieties (but we haven't counted them up). (☑682 323 714; Carrer de Provença 171; admission incl 1 drink €5; ⏱11pm-5am Fri & Sat; Ⓡ FGC Provença)

Antilla BCN
CLUB

23 Map p94, B5

The salsateca in town, this is the place to come for Cuban *son*, merengue, salsa and a whole lot more. If you don't know how to dance any of this, you may feel a little silly (as a bloke) but will probably get free lessons (if you're a lass). The guys can come back at another time and pay for lessons. (www.antillasalsa.com; Carrer d'Aragó 141; ⏱11pm-6am; Ⓜ Urgell)

Astoria
CLUB

24 🚇 Map p94, B2

Reds, roses and yellows dominate the colour scheme in this wonderful former cinema. Barcelona's beautiful people, from a range of ages, gather to drink around the central bar, dance a little and eye one another up. Some come earlier for a bite. At 9pm from Thursday to Saturday there is a 'Circus Cabaret' show with dinner (around €40). (📞93 414 47 99; www.astoriabarcelona.com; Carrer de París 193-197; admission free; ⏰9pm-2.30am Wed, Thu & Sun, to 3am Fri & Sat; Ⓜ Diagonal)

Shopping

Joan Múrria
FOOD

25 🔒 Map p94, E2

Ramon Casas designed the century-old Modernista shop-front advertisements featured at this culinary temple. For a century the gluttonous have trembled at this altar of speciality food goods from around Catalonia and beyond. (📞93 215 57 89; www.murria.cat; Carrer de Roger de Llúria 85; ⏰9am-2pm & 5-9pm Tue-Thu, 9am-9pm Fri, 10am-2pm & 5-9pm Sat; Ⓜ Passeig de Gràcia)

El Bulevard dels Antiquaris
ANTIQUES

26 🔒 Map p94, D3

More than 70 stores (most are open from 11am to 2pm and 5pm to 8.30pm) are gathered under one roof (on the floor above the more general Bulevard Rosa arcade) to offer the most varied selection of collector's pieces, ranging from old porcelain dolls through to fine crystal, from Asian antique furniture to old French goods, and from African and other ethnic art to jewellery. (📞93 215 44 99; www.bulevarddelsantiquaris.com; Passeig de Gràcia 55; ⏰9am-6pm Mon-Thu, 9am-2pm Fri & Sat; Ⓜ Passeig de Gràcia)

El Corte Inglés
DEPARTMENT STORE

27 🔒 Map p94, F4

This is now the city's only department store, with everything you'd expect, from computers to cushions, and high fashion to homewares, and famous for its decent customer service (not always the case in Spain). The top floor is occupied by a so-so restaurant with fabulous city views. El Corte Inglés has other branches, including at **Portal de l'Àngel 19-21** (Ⓜ Catalunya), **Avinguda Diagonal 617** (Ⓜ Maria Cristina) and **Avinguda Diagonal 471-473** (near Plaça de Francesc Macià; Ⓜ Hospital Clínic). (📞93 306 38 00; www.elcorteingles.es; Plaça de Catalunya 14; ⏰9.30am-9.30pm Mon-Sat; Ⓜ Catalunya)

Camper
SHOES

28 🔒 Map p94, D2

What started as a modest Mallorcan family business (the island has a long shoemaking tradition) has, over the decades, and particularly with the success of the 'bowling shoe' in the '90s, become the Clarks of Spain. The shoes, from the eminently sensible to the stylishly fashionable, are known for solid reliability and are sold all

Dry Martini cocktail bar (p103)

over the world. It now has shops all over Barcelona. (☑93 215 63 90; www.camper.com; Carrer de València 249; ☉10am-8pm Mon-Sat; Ⓜ Passeig de Gràcia)

Regia PERFUME

29 Map p94, E3

Reputed to be one of the best perfume stores in the city, and in business since 1928, Regia stocks all the name brands and also has a private **perfume museum** (☑93 216 01 21; www.museudelperfum.com; Passeig de Gràcia 39; adult/child €5/3; ☉10.30am-2pm & 4.30-8pm Mon-Fri, 11am-2pm Sat; Ⓜ Passeig de Gràcia) out the back. Regia also sells all sorts of creams, lotions and colognes. It also has its own line of bath products. (☑93

216 01 21; www.regia.es; Passeig de Gràcia 39; ☉9.30am-8.30pm Mon-Fri, 10.30am-8.30pm Sat; Ⓜ Passeig de Gràcia)

Adolfo Domínguez FASHION

30 Map p94, E3

A star of Spanish prêt-à-porter, this label produces classic men's and women's garments from quality materials. Encompassing anything from regal party gowns to kids' outfits (that might have you thinking of British aristocracy), the broad range generally oozes a conservative air, with elegant cuts that make no concessions to rebellious urban ideals. (☑93 487 41 70; www.adolfodominguez.es; Passeig de Gràcia 32; ☉10am-9pm Mon-Sat; Ⓜ Passeig de Gràcia)

Top Sights
La Sagrada Família

Getting There

Ⓜ **Metro** The easiest way to arrive, via Sagrada Família station (lines 2 and 5).

🚶 **Walk** La Sagrada Família is an easy 1.5km walk from Passeig de Gràcia.

Spain's biggest tourist attraction and a work in progress for more than a century, La Sagrada Família is a unique, extraordinary piece of architecture. Conceived as a temple as atonement for Barcelona's sins of modernity, this giant church became Gaudí's holy mission. When completed it will have a capacity for 13,000 faithful and is, in medieval fashion, a work of storytelling art. Rich in religious iconography and symbolism, at once ancient and thoroughly modern, La Sagrada Família leaves no one unmoved.

Interior, La Sagrada Família

Don't Miss

Nativity Facade

This astonishing tapestry in stone is, for now, the single most impressive feature of La Sagrada Família. Step back for an overall sense of this remarkable work, which was the first of the facades completed (in 1930), then draw near to examine the detail. It is replete with sculpted figures (Gaudí used plaster casts of local people as models) and images from nature.

Passion Facade

Symbolically facing the setting sun, the Passion Facade – stripped bare and left to speak for itself – is the austere counterpoint to the Nativity Facade's riotous decoration. From the Last Supper to his burial, Christ's story plays out in an S-shaped sequence from bottom to top. Check the cryptogram in which the numbers always add up to 33, Jesus' age at crucifixion.

A Hidden Portrait

Careful observation of the Passion Facade will reveal a special tribute from sculptor Josep Subirachs to Gaudí. The central sculptural group (below Christ crucified) shows, from right to left, Christ bearing his cross, Veronica displaying the cloth with Christ's bloody image, a pair of soldiers, and watching it all, a man called the evangelist. Subirachs used a rare photo of Gaudí, taken a couple of years before his death, as the model for the evangelist's face.

Glory Facade

The Glory Facade will be the most fanciful of them all, with a narthex boasting 16 hyperboloid lanterns topped by cones that will look something like an organ made of melting ice cream.

www.sagradafamilia.cat

Carrer de Mallorca 401

adult/senior & student/ child under 11yr €14.80/12.80/free

⊙9am-8pm Apr-Sep, to 6pm Oct-Mar

Ⓜ Sagrada Família

☑ Top Tips

▶ Jump the queue by buying tickets online.

▶ Guided 50-minute tours (€4.50) are offered throughout the day. Alternatively, pick up an audio guide (€4.50).

▶ Once inside, €4.50 gets you into lifts that rise up towers in the Nativity and Passion facades.

▶ The best time to visit is at opening time on weekdays.

✗ Take a Break

It's not often we recommend Irish pubs, but **Michael Collins Pub** (www.michaelcollinspubs. com; Plaça de la Sagrada Família 4; ⊙noon-3am; Ⓜ Sagrada Família) is an unusually authentic version of the genre, frequented by locals.

Gaudí made only general drawings of the facade, but its symbolism is clear: Christ in all His glory and the road to God.

Main Nave

In the main nave, the heart of the temple's sanctuary, pay particular attention to the columns (Gaudí used trees as inspiration), the absence of flat surfaces, and the apse (one of the earliest features to be completed) capped by pinnacles that hint at the genius Gaudí later deployed elsewhere in the church.

Crypt

From the main apse, holes in the floor allow a view down into the crypt, which was the first part of the

church to be completed in 1885. Built in a largely neo-Gothic style, it's here that Gaudí lies buried. The crypt has often been used as the main place of worship while the remainder of the church is completed.

Side Nave & Nativity Transept

The side nave, inside the door that leads beneath the Nativity Facade, is stunning with Doric-style columns and stained-glass windows. It's primarily worth visiting for the view of the main nave and its forest of columns, and of the inside of the Nativity Facade. Most people rush through here and miss one of the best interior views.

La Sagrada Família

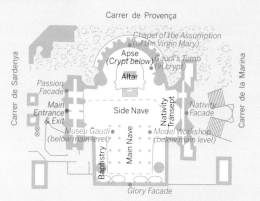

Bell Towers

The towers of the three facades represent the 12 Apostles (so far, eight have been built). Lifts whisk visitors up one tower of the Nativity and Passion Facades (the latter gets longer queues) for marvellous views. There will eventually be 18 towers – 12 Apostles, four evangelists, the Virgin Mary and Christ – which when completed will make this the world's tallest church building.

Museu Gaudí

Jammed with old photos, drawings and restored plaster models that bring Gaudí's ambitions to life, the museum also houses an extraordinarily complex plumb-line device he used to calculate his constructions. It's like journeying through the mind of the great architect. Some of the models are upside down, as that's how Gaudí worked to best study the building's form and structural balance.

Nearby: Hospital de la Santa Creu i Sant Pau

A masterpiece of Modernista style, the **Hospital de la Santa Creu i Sant Pau** (www.santpau.es; Carrer de Sant Antoni Maria Claret 167; M Hospital de Sant Pau) is a short 500m walk north of La Sagrada Família. Designed by Lluís Domènech i Montaner and completed by his son in 1930, its highlights are the 16 lavishly decorated pavilions.

Understand

Antoni Gaudí

Antoni Gaudí i Cornet (1852–1926) was born in Reus, trained initially in metalwork and obtained his architecture degree in 1878. Although part of the Modernista movement, Gaudí had a style all his own. A recurring theme was his obsession with the harmony of natural forms. Straight lines are eliminated, and the lines between real and unreal, sober and dream-drunk are all blurred. The grandeur of his vision was matched by an obsession with detail, as evidenced by his use of lifelike sculpture on the Nativity facade.

With age he became almost exclusively motivated by stark religious conviction and from 1915 he gave up all other projects to devote himself exclusively to La Sagrada Família. When he died in June 1926 (he was knocked down by a tram on Gran Via de les Corts Catalanes) less than a quarter of La Sagrada Família had been completed. It is unlikely to be finished before 2026. As Gaudí is reported to have said when questioned about the never-ending project, 'My client is not in a hurry'.

Local Life
Village Life in Gràcia

Getting There

Gràcia is a downhill walk from Park Güell.

M **Metro** Fontana station (line 3) or Joanic (line 4).

⊕ **Walk** Gràcia station is on the neighbourhood's western edge.

Located halfway between L'Eixample and Park Güell, Gràcia was a separate village until 1897, and its tight, narrow lanes and endless interlocking squares maintain a unique, almost village-like identity to this day. In places bohemian, in others rapidly gentrifying, Gràcia is Barcelona at its most eclectic, its nooks and crannies home to everything from sushi bars to badly lit old taverns.

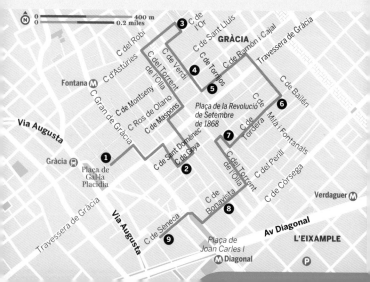

1 Local Market

Built in the 1870s and covered in fizzy Modernista style in 1893, the **Mercat de la Llibertat** (📞93 217 09 95; www.mercatllibertat.com; Plaça de la Llibertat 27; admission free; ⊘8am-8pm Mon-Fri, 8am-3pm Sat; 🚊FGC Gràcia) was designed by Francesc Berenguer i Mestres, Gaudí's long-time assistant.

2 Photo Shop

True to name, **Nostàlgic** (📞93 368 57 57; www.nostalgic.es; Carrer de Goya 18; ⊘5-8.30pm Mon, 11am-2.30pm & 5-8.30pm Tue-Sat; Ⓜ Fontana) is a beautiful space with exposed brick walls and wooden furniture specialising in all kinds of modern and vintage photography books and equipment.

3 Plaça de la Virreina

Thanks to the low-slung houses along one side and the 17th-century Església de Sant Joan on the other, Plaça de la Virreina is one of the most village-like of Gràcia's squares. With its outdoor tables, it's a lively hub for locals.

4 Local Bar

Especially welcoming in winter, **Bar Canigò** (📞93 213 30 49; Carrer de Verdi 2; ⊘10am-2am Mon-Thu, to 3am Fri & Sat; Ⓜ Fontana) is a corner bar on an animated square and a timeless locals' spot to sip a beer and chat.

5 Cafe Culture

La Nena (📞93 285 14 76; Carrer de Ramon i Cajal 36; snacks from €3; ⊘9am-10.30pm; 🚻; Ⓜ Fontana) is a neighbourhood favourite for its *suïssos* (hot chocolate) and *melindros* (spongy sweet biscuits). The area out the back is designed to keep kids busy, with toys, books and a blackboard.

6 Catalan Tradition

Catalan families in high spirits pile into **Cal Boter** (📞93 458 84 62; www.restaurantcalboter.com; Carrer de Tordera 62; mains €8-15; ⊘1-4pm & 9pm-midnight Tue-Sat, 1-4pm Sun & Mon; Ⓜ Joanic) for plates of local grub, such as the curious combination of *bolets i gambes* (mushrooms and prawns).

7 Gràcia's Tavern

If you like your taverns unchanged for years, with huge old wine barrels and a motley crew of punters, **Raïm** (Carrer del Progrés 48; ⊘7pm-2.30am; Ⓜ Diagonal) is for you. It has wall-to-wall photos of Cuba, and the *mojitos* are excellent.

8 Fashion Icon

Gorgeous **Mushi Mushi** (📞93 292 29 74; www.mushimushicollection.com; Carrer de Bonavista 12; ⊘4.30-8.30pm Mon, 11am-3pm & 4.30-8.30pm Tue-Sat; Ⓜ Fontana) specialises in quirky but elegant women's fashion and accessories. The collection changes frequently, so a return visit can pay off.

9 New-Wave Shopping

Nobodinoz (www.nobodinoz.com; Carrer de Sèneca 9; ⊘10.30am-2.30pm & 4.30-8.30pm Mon-Sat; Ⓜ Diagonal) claims to be Spain's first concept store for kids. The toys, clothes, furnishings and knick-knacks range from vintage to modern chic.

Top Sights
Park Güell

Getting There

🅜 **Metro** The walk to the park is signposted from both Vallcarca and Lesseps stations (both line 3).

🚌 **Bus** Bus 24 drops you at an entrance near the top of the park.

One of Antoni Gaudí's best-loved creations, Park Güell – a fantasy public park that was designed as a gated playground for Barcelona's rich – climbs a hillside north of the centre. This is where the master architect turned his hand to landscape gardening and the result is an expansive and playful stand of greenery interspersed with otherworldly structures glittering with ceramic tiles. The lasting impression is of a place where the artificial almost seems more natural than the natural.

Park Güell

Don't Miss

Stairway & Sala Hipóstila

The steps up from the entrance and the two Hansel and Gretel–style gatehouses are a mosaic of fountains, ancient Catalan symbols and a much-photographed dragon-lizard. Atop the stairs is the Sala Hipóstila, a forest of 86 Doric columns (some of them leaning at an angle and all inspired by ancient Greece); the space was intended as a market.

Banc de Trencadís

Atop the Sala Hipóstila is a broad open space; its highlight is the Banc de Trencadís, a tiled bench curving sinuously around the perimeter and alternately interpreted as a mythical serpent or, typically for Gaudí, waves in the sea. Although Gaudí was responsible for the form, the *trencadís* (broken tile) surface designs were the work of Gaudí's right-hand man, Josep Maria Jujol.

Casa-Museu Gaudí

The spired house east of the Banc de Trencadís is the **Casa-Museu Gaudí** (www.casamuseugaudi. org; adult/senior & student €5.50/4.50; ☉10am-8pm), where Gaudí lived for most of his last 20 years (1906–26). It contains furniture by him and other memorabilia, and its muted interior is a curious contrast to the extravagance of so many of the structures he designed.

The Viaducts

Much of the park's eastern end is dominated by the viaducts, which were Gaudí's solution to the problem of getting people and vehicles (not water) into the park. Slanting columns and local stone create an astonishing effect, seeming to spring from a fairy tale and creating the illusion that the whole structure was carved out of the mountain itself.

☎ 93 409 18 31

www.parkguell.cat

Carrer d'Olot 7

adult/child €7/4.50

☉ 8am-9.30pm daily

🚌 24 or 32, Ⓜ Lesseps or Vallcarca

☑ Top Tips

▶ If travelling by Metro, Vallcarca station is better for arriving (the uphill trek to the park is eased by escalators); Lesseps is better for leaving (it's downhill all the way).

▶ Study the details: crockery pieces adorn some sections of the Banc de Trencadís.

▶ Arrive early on weekdays and avoid weekends in summer.

✕ Take a Break

Around 1km southeast down the hill from the park entrance is **La Panxa del Bisbe** (☎ 93 213 70 49; Carrer de Rabassa 37; mains €12-15; ☉ 1.30-3.30pm & 8.30pm-midnight Tue-Sat; Ⓜ Joanic), a highly recommended gourmet tapas haunt.

Explore

Montjuïc, Poble Sec & Sant Antoni

Looming above sea and city, Montjuïc is a lovely stand of lawns and gardens interspersed with wonderful museums and sites that took centre stage during the 1992 Olympics. At the foot of the hill lies Poble Sec, its tightly packed streets home to buzzing bars and tapas haunts. The dining and nightlife scene continues in Sant Antoni, just across Av del Paral·lel.

The Sights in a Day

☼ Before we get started, a word of warning: dining options on the hill are limited and overpriced, so pack a picnic lunch from the **Mercat de la Boqueria** (p44). However you get here (we suggest the Transbordador Aeri cable car from Barceloneta, p80), take the funicular up to the summit and work your way down. The **Castell de Montjuïc** (p126) promises marvellous views, as do the **Jardins del Mirador** (p127). Visit the **Fundació Joan Miró** (p120) before finding a quiet corner of the **Jardins de Mossèn Cinto de Verdaguer** (p127) for lunch.

☀ Spend a couple of hours at the **Museu Nacional d'Art de Catalunya** (p116), and with what's left of your time we recommend you head for **L'Anella Olímpica & Estadi Olímpic** (p126), then **Poble Espanyol** (p126) and **Fundació Fran Daurel** (p126), before descending to see what's happening at **CaixaForum** (p126).

☾ Stay long enough to catch the **Font Màgica** (p129) before heading on to **Quimet i Quimet** (p130) for delicious tapas and **Fàbrica Moritz** (p130) for cold brews. End the night back up on Montjuïc with magical views over drinks at **La Caseta Del Migdia** (p131) or dancing at **La Terrrazza** (p131).

For a local's night out in Sant Antoni and Poble Sec, see p122.

 Top Sights
Museu Nacional d'Art de Catalunya (p116)
Fundació Joan Miró (p120)

 Local Life
Nightlife in Sant Antoni & Poble Sec (p122)

 Best of Barcelona

Museums
Museu Nacional d'Art de Catalunya (p116)
Fundació Joan Miró (p120)
CaixaForum (p126)
Fundació Fran Daurel (p126)
Museu Olímpic i de l'Esport (p127)
Museu d'Arqueologia de Catalunya (p129)
Museu Etnològic (p129)

Tapas
Tickets (p130)
Quimet i Quimet (p130)
Bar Ramón (p123)

Getting There

Metro Paral·lel station (lines 2 & 3), then funicular (9am to 10pm) to Estació Parc Montjuïc (PM), where a cable car heads higher.

🚌 **Bus** Bus 50, 55 and 61, or No 193 from Plaça d'Espanya to the *castell* (castle).

Cable Car Transbordador Aeri (p80) from Torre de Sant Sebastiá in La Barceloneta to Montjuïc.

Top Sights
Museu Nacional d'Art de Catalunya

Barcelona's finest art collection looks out over the city from the Palau Nacional, the pompous centrepiece of the 1929 World Exhibition. The rich collection commences with a breathtaking selection of Romanesque art from the Pyrenees, and ends with works by Picasso and Dalí, with lavish detours into Gothic, Renaissance and baroque styles en route. Although there are many remarkable artworks here, it's the sheer breadth and scale of the collection that lives longest in the memory.

Map p124, C3

www.museunacional.cat

Mirador del Palau Nacional

adult/student/child under 16 & senior €12/8.40/free

🕐 10am-8pm Tue-Sat, to 3pm Sun

Ⓜ Espanya

Font Màgica (p129) in front of the Museu Nacional d'Art de Catalunya

Don't Miss

Romanesque Frescoes

The beautifully displayed Romanesque art section constitutes one of Europe's greatest such collections. It consists mainly of 11th- and 12th-century frescoes from churches in the Catalan Pyrenees. While it's all exceptional, the two outstanding collections are the Església de Sant Climent de Taüll frescoes (Room 7) and the Església de Santa Maria de Taüll frescoes (Room 9).

Gothic Collection

Lovers of medieval religious art will want to linger over the rich ground-floor display of Gothic art, which is dominated by deeply textured altarpieces and other works, including paintings by Catalan painters Bernat Martorell and Jaume Huguet. Amid it all, seek out the sculpture *Head of Christ* by Jaume Cascalls, a haunting bust dating from 1352.

El Greco & Fra Angelico

Before leaving the Gothic centuries and heading upstairs, two paintings warrant close and prolonged inspection. The first is *Saint Peter and Saint Paul* (1595–1600) by Doménikos Theotokópoulos, better known as El Greco. The second work is the *Madonna of Humility* (1433–35) by Fra Angelico, an idealised, near-perfect counterpoint to El Greco's slender, elongated figures.

Spanish Masters

After passing through the soaring auditorium, climb to the 1st floor, where the masters of 17th-century Spanish art make a brief appearance. Francisco de Zurbarán's *Immaculate Conception* (1632) looks out across Room 39 at his strangely disconcerting *Saint Francis of Assisi*. Nearby, Room 41 is shared by Josep de Ribera and the masterful *Saint Paul* by Velázquez (1619).

☑ Top Tips

▶ If you're visiting more Barcelona museums, consider buying ArticketBCN (see the boxed text, p50), which gives admission to this and five other museums for €30.

▶ Pick up the museum's free *Guide to the Visit* brochure, which highlights 35 masterpieces and their locations in the museum, but don't restrict yourself to these works alone.

✕ Take a Break

The cafe at the top of the steps near the entrance is fine for a coffee and a snack.

Down the hill and to the east, just off Avinguda del Paral·lel, Bodega 1900 (p122) is one of Albert Adrià's latest culinary hits, with high-end versions of classic Catalan bistro fare.

Museu Nacional d'Art de Catalunya

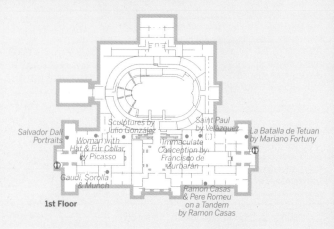

Salvador Dalí Portraits

Sculptures by Julio González

Woman with Hat & Fur Collar by Picasso

Saint Paul by Velázquez

Immaculate Conception by Francisco de Zurbarán

La Batalla de Tetuan by Mariano Fortuny

Gaudí, Sorolla & Munch

Ramon Casas & Pere Romeu on a Tandem by Ramon Casas

1st Floor

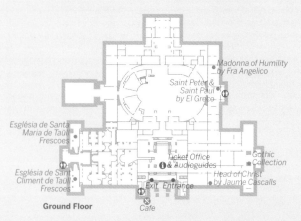

Madonna of Humility by Fra Angelico

Saint Peter & Saint Paul by El Greco

Església de Santa Maria de Taüll Frescoes

Església de Sant Climent de Taüll Frescoes

Ticket Office & Audioguides

Gothic Collection

Head of Christ by Jaume Cascalls

Exit Entrance

Cafe

Ground Floor

Catalan Masters

The 1st floor is dominated by Catalan painters and offers an intriguing insight into artists little known beyond Catalonia. There's much to turn the head, but our highlights are Mariano Fortuny's *La Batalla de Tetuan* (1863–73) and the works of Modernista painter Ramon Casas (1866–1932), especially *Ramon Casas and Pere Romeu on a Tandem* (1897).

Gaudí, Sorolla & Munch

Some furniture pieces by Antoni Gaudí and Joaquim Mir (1873–1940) continue the Catalan theme – the latter's *Terraced Village* (1909) is a lovely work. But dropped down amid this relatively uniform collection of Catalan art are two works by undoubted European masters: Valencian painter Joaquín Sorolla and Norwegian Edvard Munch.

Picasso & Dalí

Two sober works by Salvador Dalí – *Portrait of my Father* (1925) and *Portrait of Joan Maria Torres* (1921) – are what everyone comes to see, but fans of Picasso are rewarded by a handful of paintings, among them the cubist *Woman with Hat and Fur Collar* (1937), which is one of the museum's standout pieces.

JOHN HARPER/GETTY IMAGES ©

Statuary at the Museu Nacional d'Art de Catalunya

Julio González

Having checked off the big names, most visitors head for the exit, but we recommend you stay long enough to appreciate the beautiful sculptures by Julio González (1876–1942), Catalonia's premier 20th-century sculptor. His abstract human forms, such as those in *Still Life II* (1929), have a slender grace.

Top Sights
Fundació Joan Miró

Dedicated to one of the greatest artists to emerge in Barcelona in the 20th century, Joan Miró (1893–1983), this outstanding gallery is a must-see. The foundation holds the greatest single collection of the artist's work, comprising around 220 of his paintings, 180 sculptures, some textiles and more than 8000 drawings. Only a smallish portion is ever on display, but there's always a representative sample from his early paintings through to a master in full command of his unique style.

Map p124, E3

www.fundaciomiro-bcn.org

Parc de Montjuïc

adult/child €11/free

⊙10am-8pm Tue-Sat, to 9.30pm Thu, to 2.30pm Sun & holidays

🚍55, 150, funicular Paral·lel

Fundació Joan Miró

Don't Miss

The Formative Years

Room 16 The young Joan Miró began, like most masters, by painting figurative forms, but his move to Paris in 1920 prompted a shift to the avant-garde styles that he would make his own. His 1925 work *Painting (The White Glove)* has that unmistakable Miró sense of the artist having taken everything apart and reassembled it on a whim.

The War Years

Room 17 Miró spent most of the Spanish Civil War (1936–39) in exile in France, and his works from this period are uncharacteristically dark. During WWII, his approach to painting changed, reflecting a desire to escape reality, as highlighted in the bold colours and childlike figures of *The Morning Star* (1940) and *Woman Dreaming of Escape* (1945).

1960s & Paper

Rooms 19 & 20 After soaking up the vivid colours of Miró's 1960s paintings in Room 19 – linger over *Painting (for Emil Fernandez Miró)* from 1963 and *Catalan Peasant in the Moonlight* (1968) in particular – pause in Room 20. This is where Miró's love of painting on paper, and the flexibility it offered, is showcased with paintings that span five decades.

Col·lecció Katsuta

Rooms 21 & 22 This far-reaching private collection of Miró's works feels like an unexpected bonus at exhibition's end. It's a reprise of his career from the sober Catalan landscapes of his youth (such as *Landscape, Mont-Roig* in Room 21) through to the masterful and enigmatic *The Smile of a Tear* (1973) in Room 22.

☑ Top Tips

▶ If you're visiting more Barcelona museums, consider buying ArticketBCN (see the boxed text, p50), which gives admission to this and five other museums for €30.

▶ Don't miss the basement *Homenatge a Joan Miró* (Homage to Joan Miró), with works by Henry Moore, Antoni Tàpies and Eduardo Chillida.

▶ Pay for the audioguide – it's worth every euro.

✗ Take a Break

There's a small cafe selling snacks in the museum – it's nothing special, but you're not spoiled for choice in Montjuïc.

One of our favourite tapas bars in Barcelona, Quimet i Quimet (p130) is close to the bottom of the funicular station down in Poble Sec.

Q Local Life
Nightlife in Sant Antoni & Poble Sec

For locals, the area of Poble Sec and neighbouring Sant Antoni is the hot destination of the moment, with a buzzing array of cafes, bars and eateries drawing young, hip crowds to this once sleepy corner of Barcelona. This route starts off with some tapas bar snacking, before moving on to more serious drinking dens and nightspots.

❶ Culinary Superstar
The latest venture from the world-famous Adrià brothers, **Bodega 1900** (📞93 325 26 59; www.bodega1900.com; Carrer de Tamarit 91; tapas from €4.60; ⏱1-10.30pm Tue-Sat; Ⓜ Sant Antoni) mimics an old-school tapas bar, but this is no ordinary spit-and-sawdust joint. Witness, for example, the simply exquisite *mollete de calamars,* served piping hot from the oven with chipotle mayonnaise, kim chi and lemon zest.

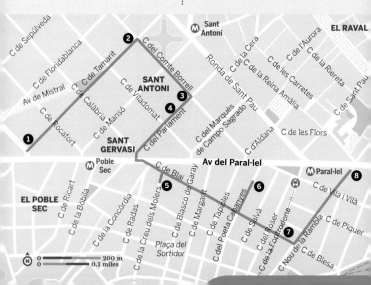

❷ Tapas & Rock 'n' Roll

Near the Mercat de Sant Antoni, **Bar Ramón** (Carrer del Comte Borrell 81; ⏰8pm-midnight Mon-Thu, 10am-4pm & 8pm-1am Fri & Sat; Ⓜ Sant Antoni) is a much-loved joint (opened in the 1930s) that serves up superb tapas plates. Calamari, meatballs, stuffed mushrooms, octopus – you can't go wrong.

❸ Aussie Style

On a stretch that now teems with cafes, Australian-run **Federal** (📞93 187 36 07; www.federalcafe.es; Carrer del Parlament 39; snacks from €8; ⏰8am-11pm Mon-Thu, 8am-1am Fri, 9am-1am Sat, 9am-5.30pm Sun; Ⓜ Sant Antoni) was the trailbazer, with its breezy atmosphere and superb brunches. Alongside healthy, tasty meals, cupcakes and good coffee are available all day. The leafy roof terrace makes a pleasant spot for a pick-me-up.

❹ Terrace Drinks

It bills itself as a wine bar, but actually the wine selection at **Bar Calders** (📞93 329 93 49; Carrer del Parlament 25; ⏰5pm-1.30am Mon-Thu, to 2.30am Fri, 11am-2.30am Sat, 11am-midnight Sun; Ⓜ Sant Antoni) is its weak point. As an all-day cafe and tapas bar, however, it's unbeatable. With a few tables outside on a tiny pedestrian side-street, this has become the favoured meeting point for the neighbourhood's boho element.

❺ Atmospheric Den

A succession of nooks and crannies, dotted with flea-market finds and dimly lit in violets, reds and yellows, make **Tinta Roja** (📞93 443 32 43; www.tintaroja.

cat; Carrer de la Creu dels Molers 17; ⏰8.30pm-1am Wed, to 2am Thu, to 3am Fri & Sat; Ⓜ Poble Sec) an intimate spot for a drink and an occasional show in the back.

❻ Air of Decadence

Seduction is the word that springs to mind in **Rouge Lab 2.1** (📞93 442 49 85; Carrer del Poeta Cabanyes 21; ⏰8.30pm-midnight Thu & Sun, to 3am Fri & Sat; 📶; Ⓜ Poble Sec), a bordello-red lounge-cocktail bar. The walls are laden with heavy-framed paintings, dim lamps and mirrors, and no two chairs are alike. It has many cultural events: poetry readings, theatrical shows, art exhibitions.

❼ Bohemian Bodega

At **Gran Bodega Saltó** (www.bodega salto.net; Carrer de Blesa 36; ⏰7pm-2am Mon-Wed, noon-2am Thu, noon-3am Fri & Sat, noon-midnight Sun; Ⓜ Paral·lel) the ranks of barrels give away the bar's history as a traditional bodega. Now, after a little psychedelic redecoration with odd lamps, figurines and old Chinese beer ads, it's a magnet for an eclectic barfly crowd that can get pretty lively on nights when there is live music.

❽ Dancehall Finale

The iconic **Sala Apolo** (📞93 441 40 01; www.sala-apolo.com; Carrer Nou de la Rambla 113; admission club €13-18, concerts vary; ⏰midnight-5am Sun-Thu, 12.30am-6am Fri & Sat; Ⓜ Paral·lel) is a fine old theatre, where red velvet dominates and you feel as though you're in a movie-set dancehall scene. There are concerts earlier in the evening, with DJs kicking things off after midnight.

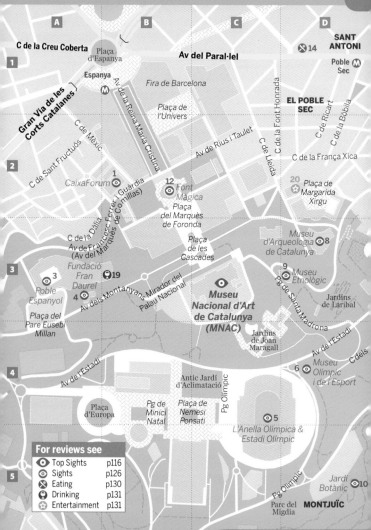

A   B   C   D

SANT ANTONI

C de la Creu Coberta

Plaça d'Espanya

Av del Paral·lel

⊗ 14

Poble Ⓜ Sec

Espanya Ⓜ

Fira de Barcelona

EL POBLE SEC

Gran Via de les Corts Catalanes

Av de la Reina Maria Cristina

C de Mèxic

C de Sant Fructuós

Plaça de l'Univers

C de la Font Honrada

C de Ricart

C de la Bòbila

Av de Rius i Taulet

C de Lleida

C de la França Xica

1

2

CaixaForum ◉ 1

C de la Dàlia

Av de Francesc Ferrer i Guàrdia (Av del Marquès de Comillas)

12 ◉ Font Màgica

Plaça del Marquès de Foronda

20 ◎ Plaça de Margarida Xirgu

Museu d'Arqueologia ◉ 8 de Catalunya

Plaça de les Cascades

9 ◉ Museu Etnològic

Pg de Santa Madrona

3

Fundació Fran Daurel ◉ 19

◎ 3 Poble Espanyol

4 ◎

Av dels Montanyans

Mirador del Palau Nacional

◉ Museu Nacional d'Art de Catalunya (MNAC)

Jardins de Laribal

Plaça del Pare Eusebi Millan

Jardins de Joan Maragall

Av de l'Estadi

C de I

4

Av de l'Estadi

Plaça d'Europa

Pg de Minici Natal

Antic Jardí d'Aclimatació

Plaça de Nemesi Ponsati

Pg Olímpic

6 ◉ Museu Olímpic i de l'Esport

◉ 5

L'Anella Olímpica & Estadi Olímpic

Jardí Botànic ◉ 10

MONTJUÏC

Pg Olímpic

Parc del Migdia

5

For reviews see	
◉ Top Sights	p116
◎ Sights	p126
⊗ Eating	p130
🍷 Drinking	p131
★ Entertainment	p131

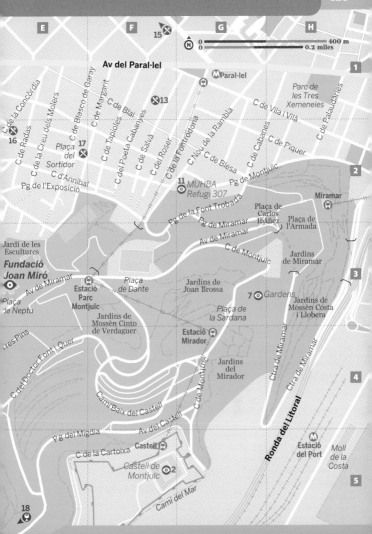

E

F

15

G

N
0   400 m
0   0.2 miles

H

1

Av del Paral·lel

M Paral·lel

Parc de
les Tres
Xemeneies

C de la Concòrdia

C de Radas

C de la Creu dels Molers

C de Blasco de Garay

C de Margarit

16

Plaça
del
Sortidor

17

C de Tapioles

C del Poeta Cabanyes

C de Blai

13

C de Salvà

C del Roser

C de la Fontrodona

C Nou de la Rambla

C de Blesa

C de Vila i Vila

C de Cabanes

C de Piquer

C de Palaudàries

C d'Annibal

Pg de l'Exposició

11 MUHBA
Refugi 307

Pg de Montjuïc

2

Pg de la Font Trobada

Plaça de
Carlos
Ibáñez

Miramar
M

Pg de Miramar

Plaça de
l'Armada

Jardí de les
Escultures

**Fundació
Joan Miró**

Av de Miramar

Av de Miramar

C de Montjuïc

Jardins
de Miramar

Plaça
de Neptú

Estació
Parc
Montjuïc

Plaça
de Dante

Jardins de
Joan Brossa

7 Gardens

Jardins de
Mossèn Costa
i Llobera

3

Tres Pins

C del Doctor Font i Quer

Jardins de
Mossèn Cinto
de Verdaguer

Plaça de
la Sardana

Estació
Mirador

Cra de Miramar

Cra de Miramar

Jardins
del
Mirador

C de Montjuïc

4

Camí Baix del Castell

Ronda del Litoral

M
Estació
del Port

Pg del Migdia

Av del Castell

C de la Cartoixa

Castell

Castell de
Montjuïc **2**

Moll
de la
Costa

5

18

Camí del Mar

Sights

CaixaForum

GALLERY

1 Map p124, B2

The Caixa building society prides itself on its involvement in (and ownership of) art, in particular all that is contemporary. Its premier art expo space in Barcelona hosts part of the bank's extensive collection from around the globe. The setting is a completely renovated former factory, the Fàbrica Casaramona, an outstanding Modernista brick structure designed by Puig i Cadafalch. From 1940 to 1993 it housed the First Squadron of the police cavalry unit – 120 horses in all. (☎93 476 86 00; www.fundacio.lacaixa.es; Avinguda de Francesc Ferrer i Guàrdia 6-8; adult/student & child €4/free, 1st Sun of month free; ⏰10am-8pm Mon-Fri, to 9pm Sat & Sun; P; MEspanya)

Castell de Montjuïc

FORTRESS, GARDENS

2 Map p124, F5

This forbidding *castell* (castle or fort) dominates the southeastern heights of Montjuïc and enjoys commanding views over the Mediterranean. It dates, in its present form, from the late 17th and 18th centuries. For most of its dark history, it has been used to watch over the city and as a political prison and killing ground. (☎93 256 44 45; www.bcn. cat/castelldemontjuic; Carretera de Montjuïc 66; adult/concessions/child €5/€3/free, free Sun pm & 1st Sun of month; ⏰10am-8pm; 🚌150, Telefèric de Montjuïc (Castell de Montjuïc))

Poble Espanyol

CULTURAL CENTRE

3 Map p124, A3

This 'Spanish Village' is both a cheesy souvenir hunters' haunt and an intriguing scrapbook of Spanish architecture built for the Spanish crafts section of the 1929 World Exhibition. You can meander from Andalucía to the Balearic Islands in the space of a couple of hours, visiting surprisingly good copies of Spain's characteristic buildings. (www. poble-espanyol.com; Avinguda de Francesc Ferrer i Guàrdia 13; adult/child €11/6.25; ⏰9am-8pm Mon, to midnight Tue-Thu & Sun, to 3am Fri, to 4am Sat; 🚌13, 23, 150, MEspanya)

Fundació Fran Daurel

MUSEUM

4 Map p124, A3

The Fundació Fran Daurel (in Poble Espanyol) is an eclectic collection of 300 works of art including sculptures, prints, ceramics and tapestries by modern artists ranging from Picasso and Miró to more contemporary figures, including Miquel Barceló. The foundation also has a sculpture garden, boasting 27 pieces, nearby and within the grounds of Poble Espanyol (look for the Montblanc gate). Runs frequent temporary exhibitions. (www.fundaciofrandaurel.com; Avinguda Francesc Ferrer i Guàrdia 13; admission free; ⏰10am-7pm)

L'Anella Olímpica & Estadi Olímpic

OLYMPIC SITE

5 Map p124, C4

L'Anella Olímpica (Olympic Ring) is the group of installations built for the

Castell de Montjuïc

main events of the 1992 Olympics. They include the **Piscines Bernat Picornell** (📞93 423 40 41; www.picornell.cat; Avinguda de l'Estadi 30-38; adult/child €6.50/4.50; ⏰6.45am-midnight Mon-Fri, 7am-9pm Sat, 7.30am-4pm Sun; 🚌50, 61 or 193), where the swimming and diving events were held and the surprisingly small 65,000-capacity Estadi Olímpic, which is open to the public when it's not in use. (Avinguda de l'Estadi; admission free; ⏰10am-8pm Apr-Sep; 🚌50, 61 or PM)

Museu Olímpic i de l'Esport
MUSEUM

6 ◉ Map p124, D4

The Museu Olímpic i de L'Esport is an information-packed interactive mu-

seum dedicated to the history of sport and the Olympic Games. After picking up tickets, you wander down a ramp that snakes below ground level and is lined with displays on the history of sport, starting with the ancients. (📞93 292 53 79; www.museuolimpicbcn. com; Avinguda de l'Estadi 60; adult/student €5.10/3.20; ⏰10am-8pm Tue-Sat, 10am-2.30pm Sun; 🚌55, 150)

Gardens
GARDENS

7 ◉ Map p124, G3

The **Jardins del Mirador** offer fine views over the port of Barcelona. Further downhill, the **Jardins de Mossèn Costa i Llobera** are of particular interest for their collection of tropical

Understand

Twentieth-Century Masters

Spain, and Catalonia in particular, produced an astonishing number of world-renowned 20th-century painters, but three stand high above the rest: Pablo Picasso, Salvador Dalí and Joan Miró.

Pablo Picasso

Born in Málaga in southern Spain, Pablo Ruiz Picasso (1881–1973) moved with his family to Barcelona in 1895. Despite spending much of his later life away from the city he returned often, and frequently said he considered Barcelona to be his true home. Picasso must have been one of the most restless artists of all time. His work underwent repeated revolutions as he passed from one creative phase to another – from his gloomy Blue Period, through the brighter Pink Period, and by the mid-1920s to dabbling with surrealism. Picasso went on to become the master of cubism, inspired by his fascination with primitivism, such as that of African masks and early Iberian sculpture. View a fine selection of his early works in Barcelona's Museu Picasso (p56).

Salvador Dalí

Separated from Picasso by barely a generation, Salvador Dalí (1904–89) started off dabbling in cubism, but quickly became identified with the surrealists. This complex character's 'hand-painted dream photographs', as he called them, are virtuoso executions brimming with detail and nightmare images dragged up from a feverish and Freud-fed imagination. Preoccupied with Picasso's fame, Dalí built himself a reputation as an outrageous showman and self-promoter. A frequent visitor to Barcelona, he was born in Figueres and spent much of his life in the seaside village of Cadaqués.

Joan Miró

Barcelona-born Joan Miró (1893–1983) developed a joyous and childlike style that earned him the epithet 'the most surrealist of us all' from the French writer André Breton. His later and best-known period is characterised by the simple use of bright colours and forms in combinations of symbols that represented women, birds (the link between earth and the heavens), stars (the unattainable heavenly world and source of imagination) and a sort of net that entraps all these levels of the cosmos. Fundació Joan Miró (p120) houses the most complete collection of his work.

and desert plants – including a forest of cacti. The beautiful, cool **Jardins de Mossèn Cinto de Verdaguer** are devoted to bulbs and aquatic plants. (☉10am-sunset; 🚌50 or PM)

Museu d'Arqueologia de Catalunya   MUSEUM

8 ◉ Map p124, D3

This museum, housed in what was the Graphic Arts palace during the 1929 World Exhibition, covers Catalonia and cultures from elsewhere in Spain. Items range from copies of pre-Neanderthal skulls to lovely Carthaginian necklaces and jewel-studded Visigothic crosses. (MAC; ☏93 423 21 49; www.mac.cat; Passeig de Santa Madrona 39-41; adult/student €4.50/3.50; ☉9.30am-7pm Tue-Sat, 10am-2.30pm Sun; Ⓜ Poble Sec)

Museu Etnològic   MUSEUM

9 ◉ Map p124, D3

Barcelona's ethnology museum presents a curious permanent collection that explores how various societies have worked down the centuries, as seen through collections of all sorts of objects. The entire museum was closed at the time of writing for major refurbishments. Check the website for reopening date. (www.museuetnologic.bcn.cat; Passeig de Santa Madrona 16-22; 🚌55)

Jardí Botànic   GARDENS

10 ◉ Map p124, D5

This botanical garden is dedicated to Mediterranean flora and has a collection of some 40,000 plants and 1500 species that thrive in areas with a climate similar to that of the Mediterranean, such as the Eastern Mediterranean, Spain (including the Balearic and Canary Islands), North Africa, Australia, California, Chile and South Africa. (www.jardibotanic.bcn.cat; Carrer del Doctor Font i Quer 2; adult/child €3.50/free; ☉10am-7pm; 🚌55, 150)

MUHBA Refugi 307   HISTORIC SITE

11 ◉ Map p124, G2

Part of the Museu d'Història de Barcelona (MUHBA), this is a shelter that dates back to the days of the Spanish Civil War. Barcelona was the city most heavily bombed from the air during the Spanish Civil War and had more than 1300 air-raid shelters. Local citizens started digging this one under a fold of Montjuïc in March 1937. (☏93 256 21 22; www.museuhistoria.bcn.cat; Carrer Nou de la Rambla 169; admission incl tour adult/child under 7yr €3.40/free; ☉tours 10.30am, 11.30am & 2.30pm Sun; Ⓜ Paral·lel)

Font Màgica   FOUNTAIN

12 ◉ Map p124, B2

A huge fountain that crowns the long sweep of the Avinguda de la Reina Maria Cristina to the grand facade of the Palau Nacional, Font Màgica is a unique performance in which the water can look like seething fireworks or a mystical cauldron of colour. (☏93 316 10 00; Avinguda de la Reina Maria Cristina; ☉every 30min 7-9pm Fri & Sat Oct-Apr, 9.30-11pm Thu-Sun May-Sep; Ⓜ Espanya)

Local Life
Culinary Lane

The pedestrianised **Carrer de Blai** (Map p124, F1) is a great place to wander in the evening. You'll find a wide range of tapas bars, cafes and restaurants, with outdoor tables on the lane. Early-evening beer-and-tapas specials draw a jovial, mostly local crowd.

Eating

Quimet i Quimet   TAPAS $$

13 🍴 Map p124, F1

Quimet i Quimet is a family-run business that has been passed down from generation to generation. There's barely space to swing a *calamar* in this bottle-lined, standing-room-only place, but it is a treat for the palate, with *montaditos* (tapas on a slice of bread) made to order. Let the folk behind the bar advise you, and order a drop of fine wine to accompany the food. (☎93 442 31 42; Carrer del Poeta Cabanyes 25; tapas €4-11; ⏱noon-4pm & 7-10.30pm Mon-Fri, noon-4pm Sat & Sun; Ⓜ Paral·lel)

Tickets   MODERN SPANISH $$$

14 🍴 Map p124, D1

This is, literally, one of the sizzling tickets in the restaurant world, a tapas bar opened by Ferran Adrià, of the legendary El Bulli, and his brother Albert. And unlike El Bulli, it's an affordable venture – if you can book a table, that is (you can only book online, and two months in advance). (www.ticketsbar.es; Avinguda del Paral·lel 164; tapas €6-15; ⏱7-11.30pm Tue-Fri, 1.30-3.30pm & 7-11.30pm Sat, closed Aug; Ⓜ Paral·lel)

Fàbrica Moritz   CATALAN $$

15 🍴 Map p124, F1

With the help of architect Jean Nouvel and chef Jordi Vilà, this microbrewery from the people behind Moritz beer has been rebuilt and opened with great fanfare as a vast food and drink complex, with wine bar and restaurant. The tapas and more substantial dishes comprise all the cornerstones of Catalan cuisine and plenty more, but be prepared to queue. (☎93 426 00 50; www.moritz.com; Ronda de Sant Antoni 41; tapas from €3.70; ⏱6am-3am; Ⓜ Sant Antoni)

Taverna Can Margarit   CATALAN $

16 🍴 Map p124, E2

For decades this former wine store has been dishing out dinner to often raucous groups. Traditional Catalan cooking is the name of the game. Surrounded by aged wine barrels, take your place at old tables and benches and perhaps order the *conejo a la jumillana* (fried rabbit served with garlic, onion, bay leaves, rosemary, mint, thyme and oregano). (☎93 177 07 40; Carrer de la Concòrdia 21; mains €8-12; ⏱9-11.30pm Mon-Sat; Ⓜ Poble Sec)

La Tomaquera   CATALAN $$

17 Map p124, E2

The waiters shout and rush about this classic place, while carafes of wine are sloshed about the long wooden tables. You can't book, so it's first in, first seated (queues are the norm). Try the house speciality of snails or go for hearty meat dishes. The occasional seafood option, such as *cassola de cigales* (crayfish hotpot), might also tempt. And cash is king. (Carrer de Margarit 58; mains €9-15; ⏱1.30-4pm & 8.30-11pm Tue-Sat, closed Aug; Ⓜ Poble Sec)

Drinking

La Caseta Del Migdia   BAR

18 Ⓟ Map p124, E5

The effort of getting to what is, for all intents and purposes, a simple *chiringuito* (makeshift cafe-bar) is well worth it. Stare out to sea over a beer or coffee by day. As sunset approaches the atmosphere changes, and lounge music wafts out over the hammocks. Walk below the walls of the Castell de Montjuïc along the dirt track or follow Passeig del Migdia – watch out for signs for the Mirador del Migdia. (☎617 956572; www.lacaseta.org; Mirador del Migdia; ⏱8pm-1am Wed & Thu, 8pm-2am Fri, noon-2am Sat, noon-1am Sun, weekends only in winter; ⓂParal·lel, funicular)

La Terrrazza   CLUB

19 Ⓟ Map p124, B3

One of the city's top summertime dance locations, La Terrrazza attracts squadrons of the beautiful people, locals and foreigners alike, for a full-on night of music and cocktails partly under the stars inside the Poble Espanyol complex. (www.laterrrazza.com; Avinguda de Francesc Ferrer i Guàrdia; admission €15-20; ⏱midnight-5am Thu, to 6am Fri & Sat, closed Oct-Apr; ⓂEspanya)

Entertainment

Teatre Mercat De Les Flors   DANCE

20 Map p124, D2

Next door to the Teatre Lliure, and together with it known as the Ciutat de Teatre (Theatre City), this is a key venue for top local and international contemporary dance acts. Dance companies perform all over Barcelona, but this spacious modern stage is the number one. (☎93 426 18 75; mercatflors.cat; Carrer de Lleida 59; admission €15-20; ⏱box office 11am-2pm & 4-7pm Mon-Fri & 1hr before show; ⓂEspanya)

Explore

Camp Nou, Pedralbes & Sarrià

The Camp Nou, home of FC Barcelona, is one of the greatest sporting temples on earth and a touchstone of Catalan identity. Up the hill to the north, village-like Sarrià belongs to a very different Barcelona. It's a refined, upmarket *barrio* (neighbourhood) that bears little resemblance to the touristy downtown area. Leafy Pedralbes nearby is home to an enchanting medieval monastery.

The Sights in a Day

☀ Like most Barcelona attractions, **Camp Nou** (p134) is a popular spot, so begin early at the ground to be able to visit the stadium and museum in relative peace. A longish walk uphill (or short cab ride) takes you to the small but splendidly landscaped **Jardins del Palau de Pedralbes** (p137). After some leafy exploration, continue to **Vivanda** (p138) for an outstanding lunch.

☀ You could easily spend a couple of hours discovering **Old Sarrià** (p138), with another hour at least to enjoy the **Museu-Monestir de Pedralbes** (p137). All this walking will have you clamouring for some nourishment for the journey – make sure you stop in at **Foix de Sarrià** (p139) for a hot chocolate fix and **Bar Tomàs** (p138) for its famed *patatas bravas*.

☾ The best way to end the night is at a lively FC Barcelona game at **Camp Nou** (p134), followed perhaps by celebratory drinks at **Lizarran** (p139). For a break from football, you could also catch a live show at long-running **Bikini** (p139).

 Top Sights

Camp Nou & the Museu del FC Barcelona (p134)

♥ **Best of Barcelona**

Eating
Vivanda (p138)

Bar Tomàs (p138)

Bangkok Cafe (p139)

Foix de Sarrià (p139)

Drinking & Live Music
Bikini (p139)

Getting There

Ⓜ **Metro** Collblanc station (line 5) is best for the Camp Nou.

FGC The easiest way to get to Sarrià (Sarrià and La Bonanova stations) and the Museu-Monestir de Pedralbes (Reina Elisenda) is by suburban train from Catalunya station in the city centre.

Ⓜ **Metro** Palau Reial station (line 3) is the best option for reaching several museums in Pedralbes.

Top Sights
Camp Nou & the Museu del FC Barcelona

FC Barcelona, the world's most successful football club, plays at the Camp Nou, a stadium well matched with the grandeur of the team's achievements. Built in 1957 and enlarged for the 1992 World Cup, the stadium holds 99,000 people and is one of the world's largest. The stadium and club are also essential pillars in understanding how Catalans see themselves. To learn what all the fuss is about, come see a game, visit the museum or take a stadium tour.

Map p136, B4

www.fcbarcelona.com

Carrer d'Aristides Maillol

adult/child €23/17

⊙10am-7.30pm Mon-Sat, to 2.30pm Sun

Ⓜ Palau Reial

FC Barcelona versus FC Internazionale Milan, Camp Nou

Don't Miss

A Real, Live Game

Tours of an empty stadium are one thing, but there's nothing like turning up to watch Barça strut their stuff live. Buying tickets is possible online, at FC Botiga shops and at tourist offices. You can also purchase by phone (☎902 189900, or 93 496 36 00 outside Spain) or at the **Camp Nou ticket office** (Gate 9; ⏰10am-6.30pm Mon-Sat, to 2.15pm Sun).

Museum

FC Barcelona's high-tech museum has an interactive mural, audiovisual displays and an astonishing collection of FC Barcelona memorabilia, from trophies (of which there are quite a few) to displays on the history of the club. Intriguingly, there are exhibits that highlight the four core values of FC Barcelona: Catalan identity, universality, social commitment and democracy.

Dressing Rooms & Pitch

The stadium tour takes you from the visitors' dressing room and out onto the hallowed turf itself. Occupying the same space that so many footballing greats have graced with their presence is inspiration enough for many, but there's also the sheer scale of this place once you walk down the players' tunnel and step onto the pitch.

FC Botiga

For some, football is the meaning of life. If you fall into that category, your idea of shopping heaven may well be this store at the football museum next to Camp Nou stadium. Here you will find footballs, shirts, scarves, socks, wallets, bags, sneakers, iPhone covers – pretty much anything you can think of, all featuring Barça's famous red-and-blue insignia.

☑ **Top Tips**

► Tickets for matches are highly sought after, but tickets for big matches are near-impossible to find, so choose matches against teams in the lower reaches of La Liga.

► There are plenty of scalpers selling tickets; make sure you're safely seated before paying up.

► Tours don't operate on match days and the museum may not be open.

► If you have a ticket for a game, get there well before kick-off to soak up the atmosphere and to make sure you find your seat in this vast stadium.

✗ **Take a Break**

There are plenty of bars in the vicinity of the stadium. A lively spot for tapas and a few beers, Lizarran (p139) is just outside Les Corts metro station.

SARRIÀ

A

B

C

D

Ronda de Dalt

Parc de l'Oreneta

C de Ramon
Miquel i Planas

Pg de la
Bonanova

C d'Iradier

C de les Escoles Pies

C de Gardúxer

C de Copèrnic
C de Freixa
C de Raset

Reina Elisenda

Pg de la Reina Elisenda
de Montcada

Plaça
de Sarrià

Sarrià

C d'Angli

Les Tres
Torres

La Bonanova

Museu-
Monestir de
Pedralbes

C del Bisbe Català

C Major
de Sarrià

C de Mañé
i Flaquer

Via Augusta

Ronda del General Mitre

C del Dr Roux

C de
Rocaberti

PEDRALBES

C de Capità Arenas

Plaça
de Sant Gregori
Taumaturg

Av de Pedralbes

Pg dels Til·lers

Parc
del Palau
Real

Jardins del Palau
de Pedralbes

Maria
Cristina

C de Bori i Fontestà

Av de Sarrià

C de Numància

Av Diagonal

Jardins de
Sant Joan
de Déu

C d'Entença

C de Jordi Girona

Plaça de la
Reina Maria
Cristina

Palau Reial

C d'Europa

C de Déu i Mata

Parc
de les
Corts

C de Nicaragua

Av Diagonal

ZONA
UNIVERSITÀRIA

Gran Via de Carles III

C de Les Corts

Plaça de
les Comes

Les
Corts

Jardins de les
Infantes

Av del Doctor Marañón

Cementiri
de Les
Corts

Av de Joan XXIII

Camp
Nou

C de Joan Güell

Plaça del
Centre

C de Berlín

LES CORTS

C d'Arístides Maillol

Travessera de Les
Corts

Jardins de
Bacardí

C de Violant d'Hongria
C de Melcior de Palau

Plaça
de Joan
Peiró

Av de Madrid

SANTS

Collblanc

Badal

C de Sants

Plaça de
Sants

LA TORRASSA

0 ────── 400 m
0 ────── 0.2 miles

For reviews see	
Top Sights	p134
Sights	p137
Eating	p138
Drinking	p139
Entertainment	p139

Museu-Monestir de Pedralbes

Sights

Museu-Monestir de Pedralbes

MONASTERY

 1 Map p136, A2

This peaceful museum provides insight into medieval monastic life. Founded in 1326, the convent is a Catalan Gothic jewel with a three-storey cloister. Visit the restored refectory, kitchen, stables, stores and infirmary. Built into the cloister walls are day cells where the nuns spent time in prayer and devotional reading. (☑93 256 34 34; www.bcn. cat/monestirpedralbes; Baixada del Monestir 9; adult/child €7/5, free 3-8pm Sun; ⏱10am-5pm Tue-Fri, to 7pm Sat, to 8pm Sun; 🚌22, 63, 64 or 75, 🚉FGC Reina Elisenda)

Jardins del Palau de Pedralbes

PARK

2 Map p136, B3

A few steps from busy Avinguda Diagonal lies this small enchanting green space. Sculptures, fountains, citrus trees, bamboo groves, fragrant eucalyptus, towering cypresses and bougainvillea-covered nooks lie scattered along the paths criss-crossing these peaceful gardens. Among the little-known treasures here are a vine-covered parabolic pergola and a gurgling fountain of Hercules, both designed by Antoni Gaudí. (Avinguda Diagonal 686; admission free; ⏱10am-8pm Apr-Oct, to 6pm Nov-Mar; Ⓜ Palau Reial)

A Wander Through Old Sarrià

Just west of Via Augusta, the old centre of Sarrià is a largely pedestrianised haven of peace. Probably founded in the 13th century and only incorporated into Barcelona in 1921, ancient Sarrià is formed around sinuous Carrer Major de Sarrià – today a mix of old and new, with a sprinkling of shops and restaurants. At its top end is pretty **Plaça de Sarrià** (Map p136, B1) As you wander downhill, duck off into Plaça del Consell de la Vila, Plaça de Sant Vicenç de Sarrià and Carrer de Rocaberti, at the end of which is the **Monestir de Santa Isabel** (Map p136, C2) with its neo-Gothic cloister.

Eating

Vivanda

CATALAN $$

 3 Map p136, B1

With a menu designed by celebrated Catalan chef Jordi Vilà, diners are in for a treat at this Sarrià classic. The changing menu showcases seasonal fare (recent selections include eggs with truffles, rice with cuttlefish, and artichokes with romesco sauce). One of Vivanda's best features is the garden-like terrace hidden behind the restaurant.

With heat lamps, it's open year-round – blankets and hot broth are distributed to diners in winter. (☎93 203 19 18; www.vivanda.cat; Carrer Major de Sarrià 134; sharing plates €9-15; ☉1.30-3.30pm Tue-Sun, 9-11pm Tue-Sat; ℞FGC Reina Elisenda)

Santana

CATALAN $$

 4 Map p136, B1

Next door to Sarrià's pretty 18th-century church (Sant Vicenç de Sarrià), Santana is an elegant spot for dining on sharing plates of seared tuna, chargrilled asparagus with romesco sauce, creative salads and steak tartar. Three-course lunch specials, including wine, cost €14. (☎93 280 36 06; Carrer Major de Sarrià 97; mains €10-17; ☉1-4pm daily, 8-11pm Mon-Sat; ℞FGC Reina Elisenda)

5° Pino

CATALAN $$

 5 Map p136, B1

While exploring Sarrià, it's worth detouring a few blocks east to this charming cafe and restaurant, which is a favourite local spot for tasty sandwiches, salads, tortillas, tapas and drinks. It's on a busy road, though the outdoor, tree-shaded terrace is still a pleasant spot for a bite. The playground next door adds to the appeal for parents with kids in tow. (Quinto Pino; ☎93 252 22 81; quintopino.es; Passeig de la Bonanova 98; mains €9-12; ☉8.30am-1.30am Mon-Fri, from 10am Sat & Sun; ℞FGC Sarrià)

Bar Tomàs

TAPAS $

 6 Map p136, B2

Many *barcelonins* have long claimed that Bar Tomàs is by far the best place in the city for *patatas bravas* (potato chunks in a slightly spicy tomato sauce), prepared here with a special variation on the traditional sauce. The place is a rough-edged bar, but that doesn't stop the well-off citizens of Sarrià piling in, particularly for lunch on weekends. (☎93 203 10 77; Carrer Major de Sarrià 49; tapas €3-5; ☺noon-4pm & 6-10pm Mon-Sat; ☒FGC Sarrià)

Bangkok Cafe — THAI $$

7 Map p136, D4

If you're craving Thai cuisine, it's well worth making the trip out to Bangkok Cafe, which serves up delectable papaya salad, steamed dumplings, crispy prawns, red curries and other classics, with more spice than you'll find in most Catalan eateries. It's a small place with an open kitchen, Formica tables and bustling crowds, but the excellent dishes for the decent prices are unbeatable. (☎93 339 32 69; Carrer d'Evarist Arnús 65; mains €9-14; ☺8-11pm daily & 1.30-3.30pm Fri-Sun, closed mid-Jul–mid-Sep; ⓜPlaça del Centre)

Foix de Sarrià — PASTELERÍA $

8 Map p136, B1

Since 1886 this exclusive pastry shop has been selling the most exquisite cakes and sweets. You can take them away or head out the back to sip tea, coffee or hot chocolate while sampling the little cakes and other wizardry.

(☎93 203 04 73; www.foixdesarria.com; Plaça de Sarrià 12-13; desserts €2-5; ☺8am-8pm; ☒FGC Reina Elisenda)

Drinking

Lizarran — BAR

9 Map p136, C4

This is a fine pre- or post-game drinking spot if you're catching an FC Barça game at Camp Nou. The beer is plentiful and cheap, there's a decent tapas selection, and on warm days you can sit on the pleasant terrace at the front. From here it's about a 15-minute walk to the stadium. (Carrer de Can Bruixa 6; ☺8am-midnight Sun-Thu, to 2am Fri & Sat; ⓜLes Corts)

Entertainment

Bikini — CLUB

10 Map p136, D3

This grand old star of the Barcelona nightlife scene has been keeping the beat since the darkest days of Franco. Every possible kind of music gets a run, from Latin and Brazilian beats to 1980s disco, depending on the night and the space you choose. (☎93 322 08 00; www.bikinibcn.com; Av Diagonal 547; admission €10-20; ☺midnight-6am Thu-Sat; ☒6, 7, 33, 34, 63, 67 or 68, ⓜEntença)

The Best of
Barcelona

Barcelona's Best Walks

The Old City in a Day 142

Modernista Barcelona. 144

Food-Lovers' Barcelona. 146

Barcelona's Best...

Restaurants 148

Shopping 150

Tapas 152

Architecture 154

Art & Design 156

Parks & Beaches 158

Sports & Activities 160

Views 161

Museums 162

For Kids 164

Tours 166

For Free 167

Bars 168

Cafes 170

Clubs 172

Gay & Lesbian 173

Live Music & the Arts 174

Bar Marsella (p47)
MATT MUNRO/LONELY PLANET ©

Best Walks
The Old City in a Day

⚡ The Walk

The triptych of Barri Gòtic, La Ribera and El Raval is where Barcelona was born. The Barri Gòtic is the old city's heart and soul, while El Raval is a vibrant mix of vintage storefronts and immigrant arrivistes. La Ribera, with El Born, is quintessential Barcelona – an icon of cool, but home to attractions of more enduring legacy. This walk takes you through these areas, past fabulous museums, monuments to antiquity, intimate squares and along the irresistible La Rambla.

Start Museu Picasso; Ⓜ Jaume I

Finish Museu d'Art Contemporani de Barcelona; Ⓜ Universitat

Length 2.5km; two hours

✖ Take a Break

Art deco and bohemian, **Cafè de L'Òpera** (p40) has had a front-row seat on La Rambla since 1929 and is the perfect old-city rest stop.

Gothic courtyard, Museu Picasso (p56)

KRZYSZTOF DYDYNSKI/GETTY IMAGES ©

❶ Museu Picasso

The **Museu Picasso** (p56) is best visited early in the morning, making it the ideal place to begin your walk. Apart from the early Picasso paintings that so distinguish this museum, the medieval mansions that make up the gallery have been beautifully preserved.

❷ Basílica de Santa Maria del Mar

Carrer de Montcada, a typical old-city lane – narrow, boisterous and leading somewhere interesting – passes some fine tapas bars, then emerges at the lovely, shaded Passeig del Born (on your left) with the **Basílica de Santa Maria del Mar** (p60) on your right. A pinnacle of Catalan Gothic, this church is all grace, light and elegance within.

❸ La Catedral

Out the church's southwest door, the Plaça de Santa Maria del Mar is a lovely little square, from which pedestrianised Carrer de l'Argenteria leads northwest to the Barri Gòtic. Pass the remnants of Roman walls, and continue on to the Gothic centre-piece of Barcelona's oldest quarter, **La Catedral** (p28), which is at once both sombre and a gilded study in excess.

❹ Plaça de Sant Josep Oriol

The **Plaça de Sant Josep Oriol** is one of the most charming squares of the Barri Gòtic. **Església de Santa Maria del Pi** (p34) looms overhead, while old shops and bars front the plaza. Outdoor tables make a fine setting for a bite or a drink.

❺ Plaça Reial

More lanes lead through the heart of the old city to the grandest of old Barcelona's squares, the **Plaça Reial** (p34), which is ringed by bars and eateries. Don't miss the wild lamp posts of early Gaudí vintage.

❻ La Rambla

Cutting through old Barcelona, **La Rambla** (p24) transports a river of people from L'Eixample to the sea. Walk northwest through this tide of people and performers before launching off its western shore into El Raval.

❼ Museu d'Art Contemporani de Barcelona

Cutting-edge galleries are a speciality in Barcelona, and the **Museu d'Art Contemporani de Barcelona** (p49) is one of the finest. Fusing a modern collection, stunning contemporary architecture and the shell of an ancient monastery, this place is Barcelona in a nutshell.

Best Walks
Modernista Barcelona

⚡ The Walk

The Modernista architecture personified by (but not restricted to) Antoni Gaudí is Barcelona's most eye-catching signature. Examples ripple out across the city, but L'Eixample has the greatest concentration. With undulating facades, otherworldly interiors, imaginative rooftops and nary a straight line in sight, Modernista L'Eixample is unlike any other cityscape on earth. This itinerary showcases why many visitors can't get enough of this breathtaking city.

Start Plaça de Catalunya; Ⓜ Catalunya

Finish La Sagrada Família; Ⓜ Sagrada Família

Length 3km; three hours

❌ Take a Break

Barcelona's tapas chefs are to contemporary cuisine what Gaudí was to early-20th-century architecture. This is exemplified at **Tapas 24** (p99).

KRZYSZTOF DYDYNSKI/GETTY IMAGES ©

Casa de les Punxes (p98)

❶ Casa Amatller

If Barcelona has a Champs Elysées equivalent, it's the Passeig de Gràcia, and close to its midpoint are some extraordinary Modernista delights. **Casa Amatller** (p96), a masterpiece by Josep Puig i Cadafalch with echoes of gabled northern Europe, is one of the standouts.

❷ Casa Batlló

You know you've arrived at **Casa Batlló** (p90) when you stumble upon dozens of passers-by gazing up at the facade with a mix of awe and amusement. Most visitors have the same reaction inside, where Gaudí turns the conception of interior space on its head.

❸ Fundació Antoni Tàpies

Designed by Domènech i Montaner, the **Fundació Antoni Tàpies** (p96) is a brick and iron building with both Islamic-inspired details and elements of pure whimsy. Note the vibrant chaos swirling over the roof, imagined by the late Antonio

Tàpies himself, whose staggering collection of paintings lies within.

❹ La Pedrera

A little further up the hill along Passeig de Gràcia, **La Pedrera** (p88) is similarly adorned with a fine facade in the best Gaudí tradition, but it's the interior (the attic is like inhabiting a fossil, the apartment like inhabiting a dream) and the rooftop that transform this apartment building into the realm of genius.

❺ Palau del Baró Quadras

The Modernistas were inspired by everything from Gothic to Orientalist styles and you'll find all of these on show in the **Palau del Baró Quadras** (p98). It's the work of Puig i Cadafalch, a towering Modernista genius.

❻ Casa de les Punxes

Nowhere does the Modernista aesthetic intersect so clearly with the childlike evocation of a fairy tale than in Puig i Cadafalch's **Casa de les Punxes** (p98). Turrets

resemble witches' hats in this castle-like flight of neo-Gothic fancy.

❼ La Sagrada Família

Nothing compares to **La Sagrada Família** (p107). Gaudí's unfin-

ished masterwork is quite simply one of the world's foremost architectural creations, at once the high point of the Modernista style and a work so utterly original as to deserve a category of its own.

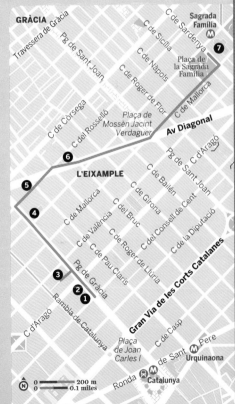

Best Walks
Food-Lovers' Barcelona

✪ The Walk

Barcelona is synonymous with food of the highest quality and the ways to sample this are seemingly endless, from ageless tapas bars and Michelin-starred restaurants to roiling markets and corner shops that have been selling the finest local products for more than a century. Food in this city is a way of life and one of the more pleasurable ways to enter into the local culture. This walk begins that process of initiation.

Start Quimet i Quimet; **M** Paral·lel

Finish Comerç 24; **M** Arc de Triomf

Length 3.5km; three to four hours

✪ Take a Break

In a medieval-like setting in Barri Gòtic, the **Cafè de l'Acadèmia** (p35) serves outstanding Catalan fare, and you can dine out on the plaza on warm sunny days.

Mercat de la Boqueria (p44)

❶ Quimet i Quimet

Choosing our favourite tapas bar in a city that's world-famous for them is no easy task, but **Quimet i Quimet** (p130) would always make the shortlist. Catalan tapas *par excellence*, bottles of every alcoholic beverage imaginable and an agreeable atmosphere built up over five generations are a near-perfect recipe.

❷ Granja M Viader

Barcelona's tradition of milk bars finds its most famous expression in the timeless **Granja M Viader** (p47) in El Raval. Its milk-chocolate drinks are renowned and the ambience is a cross between American diner and 19th-century Barcelona.

❸ Mercat de la Boqueria

Barcelona's best market, **Mercat de la Boqueria** (p44), is the most easily accessible of all Barcelona's culinary traditions. It's here that the city's celebrated chefs do their shopping, and it's all about colour, quality and people who take their food seriously.

❹ Caelum

One peculiarity of Spanish cuisine is the food that emerges from convents all across the country. Many of these items have been packaged up, along with other rare and artisan-made delicacies, and offered for sale at **Caelum** (p41). Stay long enough for a coffee in the medieval basement.

❺ Fires, Festes i Tradicions

Barcelona offers numerous antidotes to fast food and **Fires, Festes i Tradicions** (p41) is a wonderful shop window for delectable goodies from Catalonia. You'll find cheese, smoked meats, jams and other temptations. Browse an even greater selection of cheese across the street at **Formatgeria La Seu**.

❻ Hofmann Pastisseria

No matter the time of day, it's never the wrong moment to bite into a plump raspberry-filled croissant, crispy hazelnut cookie or a decadent cake, provided they come from

Hofmann Pastisseria (p72). Get a few treats to go, and devour them on the Passeig del Born.

❼ Comerç 24

Places like **Comerç 24** (p69) is the tip of Barcelona's culinary

crescendo, taking traditional recipes developed over centuries and transforming them. It's chic, the proud owner of a Michelin star, and a wonderful place to rest at journey's end. Book ahead.

Best
Restaurants

Barcelona is one of Europe's richest culinary capitals and there are few corners of the city where you can't find highly regarded cuisine. Traditional Catalan is the mainstay, but there are also ultramodern designer temples to gastronomic experimentation and places serving dishes from the rest of Spain. For the best tapas, see p152.

ROBERT GEORGE YOUNG/GETTY IMAGES ©

New Wave Catalan

Avant-garde chefs have made Catalonia famous throughout the world for their food laboratories, their commitment to food as art and their crazy riffs on the themes of traditional local cooking. Here the notion of gourmet cuisine is deconstructed as chefs transform liquids into foams, create 'ice cream' of classic ingredients, freeze-dry foods to make concentrated powder versions and employ spherification to produce artful concoctions.

Traditional Catalan

Traditional Catalan recipes showcase the great produce of the Mediterranean: fish, prawns, cuttlefish, clams, pork, rabbit, game, olive oil and loads of garlic. Classic dishes also feature unusual pairings such as cuttlefish with chickpeas, cured pork with caviar, rabbit with prawns or goose with pears.

Seafood

There is a wealth of restaurants specialising in seafood. Not surprisingly, Barceloneta, which lies near the sea, is packed with eateries of all shapes and sizes doling out decadent paellas and deliciously grilled catch of the day. A few classic dishes to look out for include *arròs a la marinera* (seafood rice), *fideuà* (a vermicelli noodle variant of paella), *suquet* (fish stew) and *bollabessa de peix i marisc* (fish and seafood bouillabaisse).

Best Traditional Catalan

Cafè de l'Acadèmia Superb Catalan gastronomy in an enchanting Barri Gòtic setting. (p35)

Suculent High-quality traditional recipes from culinary superstar Carles Abellan. (p51)

Mam i Teca Catalan cooking done right in El Raval. (p50)

Casa Calvet A memorable feast dining in a Gaudí building. (p101)

Vivanda Magnificent Catalan cooking with year-round dining in the garden. (p138)

Taverna Can Margarit Long-running eatery serving rabbit and other classic dishes. (p130)

Vinateria del Call Romantic medieval setting

for decadent traditional recipes. (p36)

Best Seafood

Passadís del Pep Well-kept local secret for the freshest seafood in Barcelona. (p69)

Barraca Mouth-watering paellas and rice dishes at this newish seafront favourite. (p82)

Can Majó Unbeatable combo of rich *suquets* (fish stews) and outdoor dining near the water. (p82)

Can Maño Humble-looking tavern that serves excellent seafood at affordable prices. (p82)

Best New Wave

Cinc Sentits Michelin-starred and a laboratory for creative cookery. (p98)

Comerç 24 Another Michelin star, another showcase for delicious experimentation. (p69)

Allium Seasonal organic cuisine with unique twists on Catalan recipes. (p38)

Pla Old-style set-ting, new-style taste combinations with

discernible roots in local traditions. (p36)

Best Vegetarian

Rasoterra Creative vegetarian dishes with a wide range of European and Eastern influences. (p36)

Sésamo Probably Bar-celona's best vegetarian restaurant, with out-standing tapas. (p51)

Amaltea A much-loved meat-free eatery in L'Eixample. (p102)

Best International

Koy Shunka Dine at the wraparound counter and watch the master sushi chefs prepare morsels of perfection. (p36)

El Atril Aussie-influenced menu (including kanga-roo fillet) and outdoor dining. (p69)

Bangkok Cafe Hands down Barcelona's best Southeast Asian cooking. (p139)

En Aparté Satisfy-ing French cuisine, plus weekend brunch. (p70)

Casa Delfín Delicious Mediterranean fare served in an atmospheric setting. (p63)

Best Desserts

Cremeria Toscana Offers some of Barcelona's finest gelato. (p102)

Caelum Dine on sweet perfection in the pleasant cafe, or head downstairs for medieval atmosphere. (p41)

 Worth a Trip

Northwest of Bar-celoneta in Poble-nou, **Can Recasens** (📞 93 300 81 23; Rambla del Poblenou 102; mains €6-14; h9pm-1am Mon-Sat & 1-4pm Sat; M Poblenou) hides a warren of warmly lit rooms full of oil paintings and fairy lights. The food is outstanding, with a mix of salads, fon-dues, smoked meats, cheeses and open-faced sandwiches piled high with delicacies like wild mushrooms and brie or *escalivada* (grilled vegetables) and gruyere.

Best
Shopping

A world-class shopping destination, Barcelona's sense of style pervades everything from fashion and home accessories to food shops, markets, antiques and handicrafts. Fashion's true home is L'Eixample and the streets surrounding the iconic Passeig de Gràcia. Elsewhere, boutiques in narrow old-city lanes make you feel like you've stumbled upon hidden treasure.

DIEGO LEZAMA/GETTY IMAGES ©

Fashion

You'll find boutiques devoted to the big Spanish designers alongside respected Catalan designers, such as the enduring Armand Basi and the celebrated and youthful Custo Dalmau. And there's barely an international brand that doesn't have an outlet in Barcelona. The grid-like streets in the heart of L'Eixample – known as the Quadrat d'Or (Golden Square) – offer the richest pickings.

Food & Drink

Produce markets may grab the attention – the Mercat de la Boqueria could be Europe's finest – but Barcelona is also studded with little gourmet food stores, some unchanged in a century, others riding some new wave as is the Barcelona way. They're the perfect places to shop for a picnic or souvenirs.

Antiques & Homewares

Barcelona's old city – the Barri Gòtic, La Ribera and El Raval – are splendid places to set off on a treasure hunt, because it's in these twisting lanes that traditions survive, whether in the form of antiques, quirky local crafts or retro furnishings. At the other end of the spectrum there's Vinçon, Barcelona's cutting-edge purveyor of slick designer homewares in every imaginable form.

Best Fashion & Design Shops

Custo Barcelona Barcelona's most dynamic home-grown brand with outrageous cuts and colours. (p72)

Coquette Offbeat women's clothes designers who share an ethereal elegance. (p73)

Loisaida Men and women's fashion, antiques and retro vinyl. (p72)

Lurdes Bergada Top-notch design and muted tones. (p93)

Camper Casual but classy shoes from the world-famous Mallorcan brand. (p104)

Bagués-Masriera Where else could you find jewellery crafted into Modernista forms? (p93)

El Raval (42)

Best Food & Drink Shops

Mercat de la Boqueria
Fresh food market and mother lode of Barcelona's culinary culture. (p44)

Caelum Sweets, preserves and convent-cooked cookies from all over Spain. (p41)

Fires, Festes i Tradicions Gorgeously packed Catalan specialities, from quince jelly to charcuterie. (p41)

Olisoliva Olive oils and vinegars from across the country. (p73)

Cacao Sampaka
Chocolate-lovers shouldn't miss this L'Eixample beauty. (p93)

Casa Gispert Roast nuts of every type, plus chocolate, conserves and olive oils. (p72)

Vila Viniteca A jaw-dropping cathedral of wines. (p73)

Foix de Sarrià Artfully made cakes and pastries that look almost too good to eat. (p139)

Joan Múrria The finest edible products from Catalonia and elsewhere in Spain. (p104)

Best Antiques & Homewares

Port Antic A small but lively weekend antiques market near the end of La Rambla. (p82)

El Bulevard dels Antiquaris A labyrinth of tiny antique shops that merits a morning's browsing. (p104)

Vinçon The standard by which Catalan design is judged. (p92)

Worth a Trip

Barcelona's most authentic flea market, **Els Encants Vells** (Fira de Bellcaire; ☎93 246 30 30; www.encantsbcn.com; Plaça de les Glòries Catalanes; ⏰8am-8pm Mon, Wed, Fri & Sat; Ⓜ Glòries), northeast of L'Eixample, is where bargain-hunters rifle through everything from battered old shoes and bric-a-brac to antique furniture and new clothes. Go in the morning for the best choice.

Best
Tapas

Tapas, those bite-sized morsels of genius, are an essential pillar in Barcelona's culinary culture. Like all elements of Catalan cuisine, the breadth of choice when it comes to tapas is extraordinary, from the traditional Catalan way of serving seafood from a can to astonishing little taste combinations whose origins lie in a laboratory.

MICHAEL HEFFERNAN/LONELY PLANET ©

Eating & Drinking

As per the 'bar' designation, these places are less formal than restaurants, and drinking is an essential component in the experience. Indeed tapas eating often happens on bar stools, or sometimes standing around at counters. Given much of the food is ready to eat when you arrive, the tapas bar makes a good option if you want something in a hurry, or hit a few tapas spots on a bar crawl around town.

How to Tapas

Ordering tapas generally works like this: you take your seat at the bar or one of the cafe-style tables usually on hand, order drinks – try the *txacolí* (slightly fizzy white wine), a glass of *cava*, a house-made *vermut* (vermouth) or a refreshing *caña* (draft beer) – and ask for a plate. Some places merely have plates stacked up, and you help yourself.

Many of the tapas are *montaditos* (a sort of canapé), which can range from a creamy Roquefort-cheese-and-walnut combination to a chunk of spicy sausage. They all come with toothpicks. These facilitate their consumption, but serve another important purpose, too: when you're ready to leave, the toothpicks are counted up and the bill presented.

☑ **Top Tips**

► Tapas is best enjoyed as a predinner snack; trying to make a full meal out of it can prove expensive.

► While a tapa is a tiny serving, if you particularly like something you can have a *ración* (plate-size serving) or *media ración* (half-plate-size serving).

Best Traditional Tapas

Quimet i Quimet Award-winning morsels, home-brew beer and fifth-generation hospitality. (p130)

Cova Fumada Always packed, this down-at-the-heels spot deserves

Typical tapas dish

its neighbourhood fame. (p77)

Bar Pinotxo Pull up a bar stool at this legendary tapas joint in La Boqueria. (p51)

El Xampanyet Swirls of anchovies and a timeless atmosphere. (p63)

Elisabets Unchanged in decades and good for Catalan *fuet* (sausage) or filled rolls. (p47)

Bar Ramón Delicious small plates in an old-school, rock-loving setting. (p123)

Cal Pep Traditional with the occasional twist from this tapas haunt of long standing. (p69)

Vaso de Oro Grilled prawns as they should be, in La Barceloneta. (p77)

Jai-Ca Buzzing little Barceloneta space with excellent seafood tapas. (p82)

Bar Tomàs Down-and-dirty bar with peerless *patates braves* (roast potatoes with spiced tomato sauce). (p138)

Best Designer Tapas

Tickets Catalan cooking's first family, the Adriàs, run this temple to gastronomic goodness. (p130)

Tapas 24 Riffs on traditional tapas varieties in a slick white L'Eixample basement. (p144)

Cata 1.81 The whole world is an inspiration for the tapas here. (p99)

La Llavor dels Orígens The focus in this stylish place is Catalan regional produce. (p70)

Bormuth Serves a delightful mix of the classic and the new wave, plus tasty vermouths. (p63)

Belmonte Innovative Catalan dishes are served in a cosy setting. (p36)

Best Regional Tapas

Euskal Etxea Basque *pintxos* lined up along the bar three storeys high in El Born. (p63)

Bar del Pla Tapas from all over Spain take on new life and direction. (p63)

Best
Architecture

Few cities are defined by their architecture to quite the same extent as Barcelona. The weird-and-wonderful undulations of Antoni Gaudí's creations are echoed in countless Modernista flights of fancy across the city. But Barcelona's architecture is a multidimensional story, which begins with Gothic grandeur and continues with a spirit of contemporary innovation that adds depth to this remarkable cityscape.

Gothic Barcelona

Barcelona is one of Europe's Gothic treasure chests, and it was largely from these jewels that the Modernistas took their inspiration. Catalan Gothic took its own course, with decoration used sparingly and Catalan builders championing breadth over height.

The Modernistas

Modernisme emerged in Barcelona during the 1880s, the city's belle époque. While the name suggests a rejection of the old, pioneers of the style actually delved deep into the past for inspiration, absorbed everything they could and then ripped up the rulebook. For many, Modernisme is synonymous with Gaudí (1852–1926), but he was by no means alone. Lluís Domènech i Montaner (1850–1923) and Josep Puig i Cadafalch (1867–1957) left a wealth of remarkable buildings across the city.

Contemporary Architecture

Barcelona's unrelenting openness to new ideas and the latest trends in art and design ensure local and international architects find fertile ground for adding daring new elements to the city's skyline.

RICHARD SHARROCKS/GETTY IMAGES ©

Best Gothic Giants

La Catedral The old city's Gothic centrepiece, at once extravagant and sombre. (p28)

Basílica de Santa Maria del Mar Arguably the high point of Catalan Gothic. (p60)

Església de Santa Maria del Pi A 14th-century jewel with a dazzling rose window. (p34)

Museu Marítim In the former Gothic shipyards just off the seaward end of La Rambla. (p81)

Museu-Monestir de Pedralbes A 14th-century monastery with a superb three-level cloister. (p137)

Museu Picasso Rare surviving examples of Gothic mansions, now converted artfully into exhibition space. (p56)

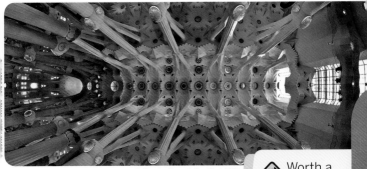

Ceiling, La Sagrada Família (p106)

Best of Gaudí

La Sagrada Família
Gaudí's unfinished symphony. (p107)

La Pedrera Showpiece
Gaudí apartment building
with an otherworldly roof.
(p88)

Casa Batlló An eye-catching facade, with an
astonishing interior to
match (p90)

Palau Güell Recently
reopened and a match
for Gaudí's better-known
works elsewhere. (p49)

Park Güell Gaudí's playfulness in full swing. (p113)

Best of the Modernista Rest

Palau de la Música Catalana Breathtaking concert
hall by Lluís Domènech i
Montaner. (p71)

Casa Amatller Josep Puig
i Cadafalch's neighbour
to Casa Batlló with gabled
roof. (p96)

Casa Lleó Morera
Ornate facade of dancing
nymphs, rooftop cupolas
and interior stained glass.
(p96)

Fundació Antoni Tàpies
A brick and iron-framed
masterpiece designed by
Domènech i Montaner.
(p96)

**Hospital de la Santa
Creu i Sant Pau** Gilded
pavilions north of La
Sagrada Família by Lluís
Domènech i Montaner.
(p109)

Palau del Baró Quadras
Stained-glass and neo-Gothic flourishes by
Josep Puig i Cadafalch.
(p98)

Worth a Trip

Nicknamed *la grapadora* (the stapler) by locals, the brand-new **Museu del Disseny de Barcelona** (☎ 93 256 68 00; www.museu deldisseny.cat; Plaça de les Glòries Catalanes 37; Ⓜ Glòries) has geometric facades and a rather brutalist appearance. Nearby is Barcelona's very own cucumber-shaped tower, Jean Nouvel's luminous **Torre Agbar** (www. torreagbar.com; Avinguda Diagonal 225; Ⓜ Glòries) soon to be transformed into a luxury hotel.

Best
Art & Design

CARLOS SANCHEZ PEREYRA/GETTY IMAGES ©

Barcelona has for centuries been a canvas for great Spanish and Catalan artists – its streets, squares, parks and galleries are littered with the signatures of artists past and present. From Modernista sculptors, such as Josep Llimona, to international and home-grown stars, such as Roy Lichtenstein and Joan Miró, they've all left their mark.

Street Art

Since the return of democracy in the late 1970s, the town hall has not been shy about encouraging the placement of sometimes grandiose and often incomprehensible contemporary works in the city's public spaces. Among the works *barcelonins* regularly encounter: Frank Gehry's fish sculpture, which they walk beneath en route to Port Olímpic; a Miró mosaic on La Rambla; and a rather baffling Tàpies sculpture on the edge of Parc de la Ciutadella. There's even a soaring sculpture of intertwined wires, which pays homage to *castellers* (human castles), near city hall in the Plaça de Sant Miquel.

Twentieth-Century Art

Two great names in 20th-century art – Pablo Picasso and Joan Miró – had strong ties to Barcelona, and both left considerable legacies in the city. Pivotal artwork from Picasso's early days is on show here, as is the most complete collection of Joan Miró's masterworks. Aside from these international figures, Barcelona has been a minor cauldron of activity, dominated by figures such as Antoni Tàpies. Early in his career (from the mid-1940s onwards) he seemed keen on self-portraits, but also experimented with collage using materials from wood to rice.

Best 20th-Century Art & Design

Museu Picasso A journey through Picasso's work before cubism took over his life. (p56)

Fundació Joan Miró Joan Miró's portfolio, from his formative years to later works. (p120)

Fundació Antoni Tàpies A selection of Tàpies' works and contemporary art exhibitions. (p96)

Museu Nacional d'Art de Catalunya Modern Catalan art on the 1st floor of Barcelona's premier art museum. (p116)

Museu d'Art Contemporani de Barcelona Fabulous rotating collection of local and international contemporary art. (p49)

CaixaForum (p126)

Fundació Suñol Rich private collection of photography, sculpture and paintings (some by Picasso). (p98)

Centre de Cultura Contemporània de Barcelona High-class rotating exhibitions, often focusing on photography. (p50)

CaixaForum Dynamic artistic space in a beautifully converted Modernista building. (p126)

Museu del Modernisme Català Modernistas (including Gaudí) turn their attention to home furnishings. (p97)

Best Street Art

Homenatge a la Barceloneta Rebecca Horn's tribute to La Barceloneta's pre-Olympics waterfront culture. (p80)

Mosaïc de Miró The work of Barcelona's artistic icon adorns the footpath of La Rambla. (p26)

Gaudí's Lamp Posts One of Gaudí's earliest commissions in the Barri Gòtic's Plaça Reial. (p34)

Worth a Trip

Situated behind the bullring and close to Plaça Espanya, the **Parc de Joan Miró** (Carrer de Tarragona) was created in the 1980s and is well worth the quick detour to see Miró's phallic sculpture titled *Dona i Ocell* (Woman and Bird).

Best
Parks & Beaches

The tight tangle of lanes that constitutes Barcelona's old town can feel claustrophobic at times. But once you move beyond, Barcelona opens up as a city of light and space – its parks, gardens and long stretches of sand bequeathing the city an unmistakably Mediterranean air. Locals love nothing better than to immerse themselves in these open areas.

JOHN HARPER/GETTY IMAGES ©

Pretty Parks & Gardens

The patchwork of parks and gardens that encircle central Barcelona to the east, west and north are much-loved focal points for local life – the ideal settings for picnics and the place to stroll, free from traffic and mass tourism. Parc de la Ciutadella and Park Güell are perhaps the best-known stands of green, but Montjuïc, on the steep rise that overlooks Barcelona from the west, offers the greatest variety for those looking to escape the noise of city life.

Beautiful Beaches

Barcelona's love affair with the sea began in earnest in 1992, when the development accompanying the Olympics transformed its waterfront into a sophisticated promenade. Thankfully, not all of what went before was lost and La Barceloneta retains elements of its one-time knockabout personality. It's a neighbourhood that combines those Mediterranean ideals of wonderful seafood, agreeable surrounds and a beach always close at hand. Yes, there are more beautiful beaches further along the coast, but Barcelona's city beaches are transformed by one simple fact: most lie within walking (or metro) distance of a city the world has come to love.

☑ **Top Tips**

▶ Shop for your picnic at **Mercat de Santa Caterina** (p66) en route to Parc de la Ciutadella.

▶ Ditto at Mercat de la Boqueria (p44) on the way to the gardens of Montjuïc.

▶ Eating options are sparse inside Park Güell – bring your own food here, too.

Best Parks & Gardens

Park Güell Everybody's favourite public park, where zany Gaudí flourishes meet landscape gardening. (p113)

Parc de la Ciutadella Home to parliament, a

Parc de la Ciutadella (p66)

zoo, public art and abundant shade. (p66)

Jardins de Mossèn Cinto de Verdaguer Gentle, sloping Montjuïc gardens devoted to bulbs and water lilies. (p129)

Jardí Botànic More than 40,000 plants faithful to a loosely defined Mediterranean theme. (p129)

Jardins de Mossèn Costa i Llobera An exotic stand of tropical and desert flora. (p127)

Jardins del Mirador Good views and a handful of snack bars below the castle. (p127)

Best Beaches

Platja de Nova Icària Perhaps the loveliest of Barcelona's city beaches, located just beyond Port Olímpic.

Platja de la Barceloneta Plenty of sand and more of a locals' beach than others.

Platja de Sant Sebastià Family-friendly beach where Barceloneta meets the sea.

Worth a Trip
The five **beaches** stretching northeast from Port Olímpic (starting with Platja de Nova Icària, followed by the Platja de Bogatell) have nicer sand and cleaner water. All have at least one *chiringuito* – snacks and drinks bars that are often open until 1am (late April to October).

Best
Sports & Activities

FLY AWAY WITH YOUR IMAGINATION/GETTY IMAGES ©

The Mediterranean oceanfront and rambling hilly park overlooking the city make fine settings for a bit of outdoor activity beneath the (generally) sunny skies of Barcelona. For a break from museum-hopping and overindulging at tapas bars, Barcelona has the antidote – running, swimming, cycling or simply pumping fists in the air at a never-dull FC Barça match.

Running & Cycling

Barcelona's long enticing seafront makes a fine setting for a jog or a spin, with a bike lane separate from traffic and pedestrians. Montjuïc with its fine views is another good spot for exercise. The best time to go is early morning before the crowds arrive.

Swimming & Surfing

If you like swimming in the sea, head to the beaches north of Platja Nova Icària, which are cleaner than those nearer the port. Barcelona also has some great lap-swimming options, including several waterfront sports centres

near Barceloneta. You can also surf waves off the beaches (best from October to April) or go stand-up paddleboarding year-round, with beachside rentals hiring out equipment and wetsuits.

Spas & Relaxation

A day at the spa can be a fantastic way to recharge after a few days exploring, or perhaps a few nights on the town. The best spas come replete with candlelit ante rooms and sumptuous baths and steamrooms. Most high-end hotels have spas, though the more charming options are scattered around town.

FC Barcelona match Watch Messi and co take on the world in a live game. (p134)

Piscines Bernat Picornell Swim laps at Barcelona's official Olympic pool. (p127)

Club Natació Atlètic-Barcelona Swim laps year-round at this waterfront spot. (p81)

Port Olímpic Follow the waterfront to the former Olympic port, now a yacht marina. (p77)

Boardriders Barceloneta Go surfing or try your hand at stand-up paddle boarding off Barceloneta. (p81)

Aire de Barcelona A beautiful Banys Àrabs–style spa in a historic setting in El Born. (p70)

Best
Views

Barcelona's position between sea and mountains makes for wonderful views, whether from terra firma or high above, aboard a cable car. Montjuïc and Park Güell offer multiple opportunities to look down upon this beautiful Mediterranean city, and there are lesser-known vantage points, too. Tibidabo, on the highest hill (512m) north of the city, has the best and most far-ranging views over Barcelona and out to the sea. Meanwhile, you'll find other rewarding views of the city in motion along La Rambla, from outdoor restaurants in Barceloneta and across plazas in the old city.

JOE BEYNON/GETTY IMAGES ©

Mercat de la Boqueria The best views of the market are from the Museu de l'Eròtica. (p44)

Best High-Altitude Views

Transbordador Aeri Splendid views over the whole city and along the coast. (p80)

Bell Tower, La Sagrada Família A whole new perspective on Barcelona's most celebrated work in progress. (p107)

Park Güell Sweeping city views from the Turó del Calvari in the park's southwestern corner. (p113)

Mirador a Colom This monument surveys La Rambla, the old city and the waterfront. (p27)

Castell de Montjuïc Fine views over the Montjuïc treetops to the city beyond. (p126)

Best for Iconic Barcelona

Park bench, La Rambla Watch the endlessly fascinating procession of the world's peoples. (p24)

La Pedrera rooftop Gaudí's fantastical chimney pots with stately Passeig de Gràcia behind. (p88)

Best Eating & Drinking Views

La Caseta Del Migdia An open-air charmer, hidden in the thickets of Montjuïc. (p131)

La Vinya del Senyor At night, wine in hand, beneath the floodlit Basílica de Santa Maria del Mar. (p71)

Santa Marta Sit at outdoor tables and watch the passing parade. (p85)

Best
Museums

With such a rich heritage of art and architecture, few cities rival Barcelona's array of world-class museums. As always in Spain, the line between a museum and an art gallery is deliciously blurred; in this section we've concentrated on traditional museums that take you for a ride through the history of Catalonia and beyond, with detours into the world of art.

JEAN-PIERRE LESCOURRET/GETTY IMAGES ©

History Museums

You could easily spend weeks working your way through Barcelona's museums. At journey's end, if you've visited them all, you'll have been on an extraordinarily diverse adventure through the history of Barcelona and wider Catalan region. The story of the layers of civilisation that have accumulated here, one atop the other, including the Jews and Romans, is a series of intriguing tales that add depth and context to your experience of the city. This being a port city *par excellence,* the story also leads further afield, with discourses on Barcelona's seafaring past that take in everything from Spain's former colonies to ethnological exhibits from cultures all across the world. From football to ceramics to civil war air-raid shelters, there's nowhere, it seems, that Barcelona's museums can't take you.

The History of Art

The arts loom large over so many aspects of Barcelona life, and the city's museums take up the story with aplomb. The breadth of subject matter is extraordinary, with modern architecture and Antoni Gaudí recurring themes. But where Barcelona's museums excel is in their preservation of Catalonia's unimaginably rich history of Romanesque art and architecture.

Best Journeys Through History

Museu d'Història de Barcelona Rich Roman ruins and Gothic architecture. (p34)

Museu d'Història de Catalunya A wonderfully composed ode to Catalan history. (p80)

Museu Marítim Barcelona as Mediterranean port city in the Gothic former shipyards. (p81)

Museu del FC Barcelona All the glitter of the world's favourite football club. (p135)

Museu d'Arqueologia de Catalunya Catalonia's prehistory, Visigoths and Romans. (p129)

Museu Etnològic A typically international collection of items. (p129)

CosmoCaixa

Refugi 307 Revisit wartime Barcelona in this evocative network of air-raid shelters. (p129)

Museu-Monestir de Pedralbes Window on monastic life and marvellous Gothic cloister. (p137)

Best Art History Museums

Museu Nacional d'Art de Catalunya Breathtaking Romanesque art and a peerless portfolio of Catalan artists. (p116)

Museu Frederic Marès Outstanding repository of

Spanish sculpture, with Romanesque art the star. (p34)

Museu Gaudí Step inside Gaudí's mind and workshop with drawings and scale models.

Casa-Museu Gaudí Gaudí's one-time home in Park Güell. (p113)

Museu de l'Eròtica Observe what naughtiness people have been getting up to since ancient times. (p26)

Museu Olímpic i de l'Esport Fascinating survey of Olympian history. (p127)

Worth a Trip

Kids (and many grown ups) can't resist the interactive displays and experiments in **CosmoCaixa** (Museu de la Ciència; ☎93 212 60 50; www.fundacio.lacaixa.es; Carrer de Isaac Newton 26; adult/child €4/free; ◷10am-8pm Tue-Sun; ☒60, dFGC Avinguda Tibidabo), a bright, playful science museum housed in a Modernista building at the foot of the Tibidabo hill. Think fossils, physics and an Amazonian rainforest.

Best
For Kids

From street performers who strut their stuff the length of La Rambla to art and architecture that looks like it emerged from a child's imagination, the sheer theatre of Barcelona's streets is a source of endless fascination for kids. Throw in an abundance of child-centric attractions (including beaches, pools and parks) and this is one city that seems made for a family holiday.

Child-Friendly Culture

One of the great things about Barcelona is the inclusion of children in many apparently adult activities. Going out to eat or sipping a beer on a late summer evening at a *terraza* needn't mean leaving children with minders. Locals take their kids out all the time and it's not unusual to see all ages, from toddlers to grandparents, enjoying the city until well into the night. A good starting point for what Barcelona has to offer for children can be found at www.kidsinbarcelona.com; its child-friendly listings are updated regularly.

Practical Matters

Most of the mid- and upper-range hotels in Barcelona can organise a babysitting service. Many hotels use **5 Serveis** (☎93 412 56 76; www.5serveis. com; Carrer de Pelai 50), which you can also contact directly. It has multilingual babysitters *(canguros)*. **Tender Loving Canguros** (☎647 605989; www.tlcanguros.com) offers English-speaking babysitters for a minimum of three hours. Expect to pay at least €10 an hour plus a taxi fare home for the babysitter. If you're willing to let your kid share your bed, you won't incur a supplement in hotels. Extra beds usually (though not always) incur a €20 to €30 charge.

RICHARD CUMMINS/GETTY IMAGES ©

☑ **Top Tips**

▶ Adjust your children to Barcelona time (ie late nights), otherwise they'll miss half of what's worth seeing.

▶ Ask the local tourist office for the nearest children's playgrounds.

Best Attractions

L'Aquàrium One of Spain's best aquariums with a shark tunnel and 11,000 fish. (p80)

Beaches Plenty of sand and gentle waters within walking distance.

Zoo de Barcelona More than 400 species from geckos to gorillas. (p66)

Poble Espanyol A village in miniature that's

Beatles exhibit, Museu de la Xocolata (p67)

guaranteed to capture the kids' attention. (p126)

Transbordador Aeri Exhilarating cable car that feels like a fairground ride. (p80)

Parc de la Ciutadella Central Barcelona's largest park with ample space to play. (p66)

L'Anella Olímpica & Estadi Olímpic Swim the same pool as Olympic greats. (p126)

Camp Nou The football-mad kid will never forget a visit here. (p134)

Best Museums

Museu de Cera Wax museum, complete with fairytale forest and time travel. (p27)

Museu Marítim Model ships, rafts and tall tales of the sea. (p81)

Museu de la Xocolata Every kid's dream museum. (p67)

Castell de Montjuïc Patrol the city ramparts. (p126)

Museu Olímpic i de l'Esport Sporty kids will love it. (p127)

Best for Fertile Imaginations

Park Güell Animals in glittering colours and Hansel and Gretel–like gatehouses. (p113)

Casa Batlló Architecture made for kids. (p90)

La Sagrada Família Castle-like structure that seems to spring from a medieval legend. (p107)

Fundació Joan Miró Children can relate to the childlike shapes and strong colours. (p120)

Worth a Trip

For the Ferris-wheel ride of your life, head for the **Parc d'Atraccions** (☎ 93 211 79 42; www.tibidabo.cat; Plaça de Tibidabo 3-4; adult/child €29/10.30; ⏰ closed Jan-Feb), an old-fashioned fun fair high on the Tibidabo hill. Getting here's half the fun, but always check the website for opening times before setting out.

Best
Tours

Tours certainly aren't necessary to enjoy Barcelona, but a handful of tours can enhance your visit, either by providing you with an introduction to the city or by zeroing in on an important aspect of Barcelona life that you simply couldn't access or understand on your own. Self-guided tours are another way to delve more deeply into a particular area of interest, such as the Ruta del Modernisme.

KRZYSZTOF DYDYNSKI/GETTY IMAGES ©

Barcelona Walking Tours

(📞 93 285 38 34; www.barcelonaturisme.com; Plaça de Catalunya 17-S; Ⓜ Catalunya) The tourist office runs 17 themed walking tours that focus on the Barri Gòtic, Picasso's Barcelona, Modernisme and the city's food culture.

Bike Tours Barcelona

(www.biketoursbarcelona.com; per person €22; Ⓜ Jaume I) One of numerous operators offering three-hour tours of the Barri Gòtic, waterfront, La Sagrada Família and other Gaudí landmarks. Turn up outside the tourist office on Plaça de Sant Jaume; check the website for departure times.

Las Golondrinas

(📞 93 442 31 06; www.lasgolondrinas.com; Moll de las Drassanes; 35min tour adult/child €6.80/2.60; Ⓜ Drassanes) A seaborne perspective of the city with a 1½-hour jaunt around the harbour and along the beaches to the northeast tip of town. Shorter trips available.

GoCar

(📞 93 269 17 92; www.gocartours.es; Carrer de Freixures 23; tours 2½/8 hr €70/160; ⊙ 9am-9pm) GPS-guided, two-seat, three-wheeled moped-cars with commentary as you zip around town. High on the novelty scale.

My Favourite Things

(📞 637 265405; www.myft.net; tours from €26) Offers tours for no more than 10 participants based on numerous themes: anything from design to food. Other activities include flamenco and salsa classes and bicycle rides in and out of Barcelona.

Bus Turístic

(📞 93 285 38 32; www.barcelonabusturistic.cat/en; day ticket adult/child €27/16; ⊙ 9am-8pm) This hop-on, hop-off service covers virtually all of the city's main sights. Audioguides (in 10 languages) provide running commentary on the 44 stops on the three different circuits. Each of the two main circuits takes around two hours.

Barcelona Metro Walks

Consists of seven self-guided routes, combining travel on the Metro and other public transport as well as stretches on foot. Tourist information points at Plaça de Catalunya and Plaça de Sant Jaume sell the €16 package, which includes a walks guide, two-day transport pass and map.

Best
For Free

KRZYSZTOF DYDYNSKI/GETTY IMAGES ©

There are so many museums in Barcelona that seeing even a small portion of them can seem like a major financial investment. But a series of combination tickets help keep costs down, and some of Barcelona's top attractions charge no admission, while others have free periods.

Free Days

Most government-run museums open their doors without charge on the first Sunday of every month. On other Sundays, most refrain from charging from 3pm to 8pm. And of course you pay no admission fee for attractions like markets, gardens and beaches.

Take a Walk

They're not technically free, but numerous companies offer pay-what-you-wish walking tours. These typically take in the Barri Gòtic or the Modernista sites of L'Eixample. A few recommended outfitters include Runner Bean Tours, Feel Free Tours, Discover Walks and Travel Bound. Check websites for meeting places and departure times.

Best Always Free

Basílica de Santa Maria del Mar Sublime Gothic masterpiece. (p60)

Fundació Fran Daurel Picasso, Miró, Barceló and more than 300 other works of art. (p126)

L'Anella Olímpica & Estadi Olímpic Relive unforgettable Olympic moments for nothing. (p126)

Temple Romà d'August Roman columns in old Barcelona. (p35)

Antic Hospital de la Santa Creu Wander unchallenged into the grand Gothic reading room. (p52)

Best Free Days for Top Museums

Museu Nacional d'Art de Catalunya Free 3pm to 8pm on Saturdays and all day on the first Sunday of the month. (p116)

Museu Picasso Free 3pm to 8pm every Sunday and all day on the first Sunday of the month. (p56)

Museu d'Història de Barcelona Free 3pm to 8pm every Sunday and all day on the first Sunday of the month. (p34)

Museu d'Història de Catalunya Free on the last Tuesday of the month between October and June. (p80)

CaixaForum Free on the first Sunday of the month. (p126)

La Catedral Free every day from 8am to 12.45pm and 5.15pm to 8pm. (p28)

Best
Bars

Barcelona is a nightlife-lovers' town, with an enticing spread of candlelit wine bars, old-school taverns and stylish lounges where the festivities continue late into the night. The atmosphere varies tremendously – shadowy mural-covered chambers in the medieval quarter, antique-filled converted storefronts and buzzing Modernista spaces are all part of the scene.

MATT MUNRO/LONELY PLANET ©

Bar Neighbourhoods

There are bars on just about every street corner in Barcelona, and every neighbourhood has its local watering hole. But the densest concentrations of dedicated drinking dens are to be found in Barri Gòtic, El Raval, La Ribera (particularly El Born) and L'Eixample.

Wine & Cava Bars

A growing number of wine bars scattered around the city provide a showcase for the great produce from Spain and beyond. Vine-minded spots serve a huge selection of wines by the glass, with a particular focus on stellar new vintages. A big part of the experience is having a few bites while you drink. Expect sharing plates, platters of cheese and charcuterie, and plenty of tapas.

Beach Bars

During summer small wooden beach bars, affectionately known as *chiringuitos,* open up along the strand, from Barceloneta all the way up to Platja de la Nova Mar Bella. Here you can dip your toes in the sand, grab a snack and nurse a cocktail (or a refreshing *cava sangria*) while watching the city at play against the backdrop of the Mediterranean.

Best Bars with History

Casa Almirall Barcelona's oldest continuously functioning bar with wonderful period detail. (p52)

Bar Marsella They've seen it all at this gritty 19th-century El Raval bar. (p47)

La Confitería Fin-de-siècle spot in El Raval that pours a fine house vermouth. (p52)

Les Gens Que J'Aime Romantic relic of 1960s L'Eixample with candlelight and red-velvet sofas. (p103)

Best Local Bars

Vaso de Oro Barceloneta as it used to be. (p77)

Rubí Great drink specials hidden away on a narrow lane in El Born. (p71)

Quimet i Quimet (p130)

Raïm Old wine barrels, grizzled Gràcia locals and a Cuban love affair. (p111)

Best Cocktail Bars

Boadas Cocktail favourite of Hemingway and Miró. (p51)

Dry Martini Suited waiters and perfect dry martinis in L'Eixample. (p103)

Juanra Falces White-jacketed waiters serve up artful elixirs. (p71)

Best for Style

Ocaña Sitting pretty on Plaça Reial with a beautifully designed interior. (p38)

Sor Rita Join festive crowds in a whimsical Almodóvar-esque world. (p38)

Best Wine Bars

Monvínic With over 3000 wines to choose from, you won't lack for options. (p93)

La Vinya del Senyor More than 350 wines and a perfect setting. (p71)

Best Cava Bars

El Xampanyet Nowhere does the tapas-*cava* combination better than this 1930s-era El Born bar. (p63)

Can Paixano Ageless Barceloneta *cava* den of sheer raucous pleasure. (p76)

Best Music Bars

Bar Pastís Shoebox-sized bar with music from French cabaret to tango. (p53)

Manchester Britpop from the 1980s and other UK classics. (p40)

Best Bohemian Hangouts

Gran Bodega Saltó Psychedelic decor, live music and an eclectic crowd. (p123)

Absenta Absinthe-fuelled drinking den with whimsical scultpures. (p84)

Oviso Festive anytime spot on the Plaça de George Orwell. (p39)

Tinta Roja Intimate and dimly lit with a wild showcase of live performances. (p123)

Rouge Lab 2.1 Bordello-esque bar known for its surreal performances. (p123)

Best
Cafes

Barcelona is distinguished by its historic cafes, where bow-tied waiters and period interiors are de rigeur. Many have been discovered by tourists, but you're still likely to find two men playing chess as they have done for decades, or a wizened old-timer, glass of cognac in hand, simply watching the world go by.

MATT MUNRO/LONELY PLANET ©

The Best of the Old

The Modernistas and others of their architectural ilk didn't content themselves with exotic facades: just as often, the city's architects put as much effort into adorning the interiors of the city's salons. Such is the backdrop for many a Barcelona cafe. But in this city that seems hell-bent on redefining the future, it's the atmosphere in these cafes – the clientele and the decor – that serves to remind us that this is also a profoundly traditional city. Here, an older way of doing things prevails – a mid-morning coffee or something stronger, long hours spent solving the problems of the world with friends. And therein lies the *raison d'être* of Barcelona's cafes: these are meeting places and hubs of social life, and have been for centuries.

In with the New

This being Barcelona, slick new cafes have also found a place in the affections of *barcelonins*. These are the sort of places where you sit beneath contemporary artworks as you update your Facebook profile to a soundtrack of lounge and other chill-out music, where the waiters are young and friendly, and where you're just as likely to encounter cocktails as coffee.

☑ **Top Tips**

▶ For sweet teeth, head for a *granja* (milk bar), where thick hot chocolate is the go. Cafe-lined Carrer de Petritxol in Barri Gòtic is famed for its chocolate options.

▶ A *café con leche* is a white coffee, *café solo* is an espresso and a *cortado* is an espresso with a small amount of milk.

Best Historic Cafes

Cafè de l'Òpera A grand old art-deco dame of La Rambla, going strong since 1929. (p40)

Mauri Another from the class of 1929, with an ornate fresco and classy L'Eixample clientele. (p93)

Hot chocolate and pastries

Salterio Candles and old stone walls make for a mesmerizing atmosphere at this spot in the former Jewish quarter. (p40)

Caelum Temptations of all sorts, best enjoyed in the medieval chamber in the basement. (p41)

Best Local Cafes

La Nena Hot chocolate, crêpes and desserts draw in a mix of Gràcia hipsters and young families. (p111)

Cosmo Archetypal modern art cafe – cool, chilled, and offering creative coffees and teas. (p93)

Bar Kasparo Great place to linger, with a peaceful setting overlooking a leafy plaza. (p46)

Federal Aussie-run cafe and eating spot with a pleasant roof terrace. (p123)

Best Chocolate

Granja M Viader Spain's most popular chocolate drink was invented in this 19th-century classic. (p47)

Granja La Pallaresa Leading candidate for Barcelona's best coffee or hot chocolate in the Barri Gòtic. (p31)

Foix de Sarrià A 19th-century pastry shop in Sarrià of chocolatey decadence and hot drinks. (p139)

Cacao Sampaka Chocolate lovers go weak at the knees at this L'Eixample icon. (p93)

Worth a Trip

If you're out beyond the eastern side of the Passeig de Gràcia, step a century back in time at the **Cafè del Centre** (☎ 93 488 11 01; Carrer de Girona 69; ⏰9am-11pm Mon-Fri, 11am-11pm; Ⓜ Girona). This atmospheric place, with its timber-topped bar, marble-topped tables and dark timber chairs, has been in business since 1873. The cafe exudes an almost melancholy air, but gets busy at night.

Best
Clubs

DIEGO LEZAMA/GETTY IMAGES ©

Barcelona's reputation as a party town is well deserved, although many of the better places are found in La Zona Alta, the upmarket suburbs north of the centre. If you can't move that far, there are options closer to the centre. A surprising variety of spots lurk in the old-town labyrinth, ranging from plush former dance halls to grungy subterranean venues. Along the waterfront it's another story: at Port Olímpic sun-scorched crowds of visiting yachties mix it up with tourists and a few locals at noisy, back-to-back dance bars right on the waterfront.

Best Clubs

La Terrrazza Outdoor summer-only Montjuïc venue filled with top DJs and Barcelona's beautiful people. (p131)

Moog Techno, electronica, retro pop and big-name DJs ensure a packed El Raval dance floor. (p52)

Astoria This former cinema draws the glitterati with a high-end dining room transforming into a nightclub. (p104)

Marula Cafè Best choice for a young crowd in the Barri Gòtic. (p40)

Antilla BCN Barcelona's premier club for salsa and sexy Cuban tunes. (p103)

Ocaña The downstairs lounge hosts good DJs on weekends. (p38)

La Fira Fun unpretentious crowd at this small festive nightspot in L'Eixample. (p103)

Best Live-Gig Clubs

Bikini Latin, disco, hip-hop, funk...there's something for everyone at this stalwart. (p139)

Jamboree DJ-spun hip-hop and funk on Plaça Reial. (p41)

Sala Apolo House, techno and the like with an eclectic crowd. (p123)

☑ **Top Tips**

▶ Clubs typically open from midnight to 6am Thursday to Saturday. Things are pretty dead before 2am.

▶ Cover charges range from nothing to upwards of €20. The admission price usually includes your first drink.

▶ Dress well to get past the bouncers. If you're in a big group, break into smaller groups.

▶ Browse the latest on Barcelona Rocks (www.barcelona-rocks.com), Clubbing Spain (www.clubbingspain.com) and Guía del Ocio (www. guia delocio.com).

Best
Gay & Lesbian

With a busy gay and lesbian scene, this is one of the most gay-friendly cities in southern Europe. The bulk of the action happens in 'Gaixample', the five or six blocks of L'Eixample bounded by Gran Via de les Corts Catalanes, Carrer de Balmes, Carrer del Consell de Cent and Carrer de Casanova.

LONELY PLANET / GETTY IMAGES ©

Best Bars

Dietrich Café (Carrer del Consell de Cent 255; 10.30pm-3am; MUniversitat) This cabaret-style venue shows a nightly drag-queen gala.

La Chapelle (Carrer de Muntaner 67; 4pm-2.30am; MUniversitat) Relaxed meeting place with provocative religious decor that welcomes all.

Aire (Carrer de València 236; 11pm-2.30am Thu-Sat; MPasseig de Gràcia) Popular spot for lesbians with a spacious dance floor.

Átame (Carrer del Consell de Cent 257; 10pm-2.30am; MUniversitat) Chatter over drinks early, stay late as things heat up.

Museum (Carrer de Sepúlveda 178; 11pm-3am Fri & Sat; MUniversitat) Lots of kitschy fun to be had at this so-called 'video bar'.

Punto BCN (Carrer de Muntaner 63-65; 6pm-3am; MUniversitat) A two-level bar with a good mix of ages and creeds.

Mat Bar (Carrer de Consell de Cent 245; 5pm-2am Tue-Thu & Sun, until 3am Fri & Sat; MUniversitat) Classy Aussie-run space with craft brews and bar food.

Bacon Bear (Carrer de Casanova 64; 6pm-2.30am Sun-Thu, 6pm-3am Fri & Sat; MUrgell) Burly folk and their admirers.

Best Clubs

Arena Madre (Carrer de Balmes 32; 12.30am-5am; MPasseig de Gràcia) One of the top clubs in town for boys seeking boys.

Metro (Carrer de Sepúlveda 185; 12.15am-5am Sun-Mon, until 6am Fri & Sat; MUniversitat) Top-notch DJs preside over two

☑ Top Tips

▶ Platja de Sant Miquel, south of La Barceloneta, is a gay-male nudist strip from mid-afternoon.

▶ Look out for party flyers in shops and bars in Gaixample.

▶ Most clubs open only from Thursday to Saturday nights.

▶ Find events at **60by80** (www.60by80.com) and **VisitBarcelonaGay** (www.visitbarcelonagay.com).

heaving dance floors and other amusements.

Pervert Club (Ronda de Sant Pere 19-21; midnight-6am Sat; MUrquinaona) Electronic beats and a fit young crowd.

Best
Live Music & the Arts

Barcelona is an important stop for most musicians on any European tour. Above all, watch out for local band made good Ojos de Brujo (Wizard's Eyes), who meld flamenco and rumba with rap, ragga and electronica. But even the weekly diet of jazz, leavened with a little rock, flamenco and blues, keeps locals happy.

BARBARA VAN ZANTEN/GETTY IMAGES ©

Best Live Jazz & Other Music

Harlem Jazz Club One of Barcelona's best known jazz stages, with a handy Barri Gòtic location. (p40)

Jamboree A fine jazz venue on Plaça Reial that draws big talent. (p41)

Jazz Sí Club Eclectic line-up of live music, including flamenco, Cuban jazz, rock and blues. (p47)

Sala Apolo Alternative mix of offbeat rock acts, world music and DJs. (p123)

La Pedrera Summertime concerts on the rooftop of a Gaudí masterpiece. (p88)

Bikini Features a wide-ranging program from samba to indie rock. (p139)

Plaça Nova *Sardana* (Catalan folk dancing) in front of La Catedral at 6pm Saturdays and noon Sundays.

Montjuïc Every Sunday from June through September, enjoy a day of electronic music at an outdoor space on Montjuïc (piknicelectronik.es/en).

Best High Culture

Palau de la Música Catalana Modernista auditorium, staging everything from classical music to Spanish guitar. (p71)

Gran Teatre del Liceu World-class opera, an extravagant setting and fine acoustics. (p40)

☑ **Top Tips**

▶ The Palau de la Virreina (www.lavirreina.bcn.cat) cultural information office has oodles of information on theatre, opera, classical music and more.

▶ The Guía del Ocio (www.guiadelociobcn.es; €1, or free with El País newspaper on Fridays) has ample listings for all forms of entertainment.

Survival Guide

Before You Go 176
When to Go 176
Book Your Stay 176

Arriving in Barcelona 178

Getting Around 179
Bicycle 179
Bus 179
FGC 180
Funicular.......................... 180
Metro............................. 180
Taxi.............................. 180

Essential Information 180
Business Hours.................... 180
Discount Cards.................... 181
Electricity........................ 181
Emergency 181
Money 181
Public Holidays................... 182
Safe Travel....................... 182
Telephone 182
Toilets........................... 183
Tourist Information 183
Travellers with Disabilities 183
Visas............................ 183

Language 184

Survival Guide

Before You Go

When to Go

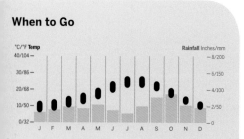

°C/°F **Temp**
40/104 —
30/86 —
20/68 —
10/50 —
0/32 —

J F M A M J J A S O N D

Rainfall Inches/mm
— 8/200
— 6/150
— 4/100
— 2/50
— 0

➡ **Summer (Jun–Aug)**
Hot beach weather,
but often overwhelmed
with visitors in July and
August; locals escape
the city in August.

➡ **Autumn (Sep–Nov)**
September is one of the
best months to visit;
chance of rain in October
and November.

➡ **Winter (Dec–Feb)**
Nights can be chilly and
there's a chance of rain,
but there are few visitors
and sunny days are
possible.

➡ **Spring (Mar–May)** A
lovely time to visit. Man-
ageable visitor numbers,
though rain is possible in
April and May.

Book Your Stay

➡ Accommodation in
Barcelona is at a premium
year-round so always
book as far in advance as
possible.

➡ Barcelona's price-to-
quality ratio is gener-
ally high, but prices can
double on weekends and
during important festivals
and trade fairs.

➡ Staying in the Barri
Gòtic, El Raval or La Ribera
puts you in the heart of
the action, but nights can
be noisy and long from
Thursday through the
weekend.

➡ L'Eixample can be
quieter, while La Barceloneta is perfect if you're here
for the beach.

Useful Websites

Lonely Planet (www.
lonelyplanet.com/spain/
barcelona) Find recom-
mended hotels and book
online.

Splendia (www.splendia.com) Good for tracking down some of the city's more striking hotels.

Barcelona Turisme (www.barcelonaturisme.com) Tourist office with a booking service covering more than 300 places to stay.

Oh-Barcelona (www.oh-barcelona.com) More than 800 hotels and apartments to choose from.

Best Budget

Alberg Hostel Itaca (www.itacahostel.com) A bright, quiet hostel near La Catedral with a lively vibe, and ample activities on offer (pub crawls, flamenco concerts, free daily walking tour).

Pensión Francia (www.pensionfrancia-barcelona.com) Quaint and clean 11-room hostel in a great location close to the shore, the Parc de la Ciutadella and El Born nightlife.

Fashion House (www.bcnfashionhouse.com) L'Eixample flat containing eight rooms of varying size done tastefully, with high ceilings, parquet floors and, in some cases, a little balcony onto the street.

Amistat Beach Hostel (www.amistatbeachhostel.com) Small, nicely designed hostel with a beanbag-filled lounge; near the beach and restaurants of Poblenou (northeast of Barceloneta).

Inout Hostel (www.inouthostel.com) Friendly, beautifully situated hostel with a strong social ethos (nearly all staff have disabilities). Restaurant and extensive facilities, but far from the centre.

Pensió 2000 (www.pensio2000.com) This family-run place has reasonably spacious doubles with mosaic-tiled floors and ensuite bathrooms. You can eat your breakfast in the little courtyard.

Best Midrange

Five Rooms (www.thefiverooms.com) Five charming L'Eixample rooms, each with a unique design. Features include broad, firm beds, stretches of exposed brick wall, restored mosaic tiles and minimalist decor.

Hotel Banys Orientals (www.hotelbanysorientals.com) This magnetically popular designer haunt has small rooms done up in cool blues and aquamarines, combined with dark-hued floors.

Chic & Basic Ramblas (www.chicandbasicramblashotel.com) Quirky and arty, with a vintage auto in the lobby and colourful rooms that loosely pay homage to Barcelona life circa 1960. All have balconies and small kitchens.

Hotel Sant Agustí (www.hotelsa.com) Just off La Rambla, this former 18th-century monastery has sparkling rooms that are mostly spacious and light-filled.

Cami Bed & Gallery (www.camibedandgallery.com) In a handsome Modernista building near Plaça Catalunya, this luxury B&B has airy rooms, with high ceilings and handsome design touches, though only one has a private bathroom.

Hotel Constanza (www.hotelconstanza.com) A boutique beauty with lovely rooms and fine L'Eixample views from the roof terrace.

Best Top End

Hotel Neri (www.hotelneri.com) Stunningly renovated medieval mansion overlooking one of Barcelona's most peaceful squares.

DO (www.hoteldoreial.com) Handsomely designed rooms, roof terrace (with bar in summer), dipping pool, spa and market-to-table restaurant.

Hotel Mercer (www.mercerbarcelona.com) Lavish designer rooms with medieval elements, plus an interior garden, rooftop dip pool, stylish cocktail lounge and top-notch restaurant.

Casa Camper (www.casacamper.com) Museum-like foyer and stylish rooms with Vinçon furniture and design smarts. The rooftop has sweeping city views.

Hotel Casa Fuster (www.hotelcasafuster.com) This sumptuous Modernista mansion has small plush rooms with period features.

Best Short-Stay Apartments

Airbnb (www.airbnb.com) Browse hundreds of listings of spare rooms or entire apartments that locals rent out across the city. Prices per night in a decent area start at around €30 for a room and €75 for an apartment.

Aparteasy (www.aparteasy.com) Excellent range of centrally located apartments ranking from small and dated to large and luxurious.

Feel at Home Barcelona (www.feelathomebarcelona.com) Small select group of rentals in La Rambla, El Raval and Sarrià.

Friendly Rentals (www.friendlyrentals.com) Dozens of high-quality options across the city from this experienced operator.

Arriving in Barcelona

☑ **Top Tip** For the best way to get to your accommodation, see p17.

Aeroport del Prat

Barcelona's **El Prat Airport** (☎902 404074; www.aena.es) lies 17km southwest of Plaça de Catalunya. The airport has two main terminal buildings: the new T1 terminal and the older T2, itself divided into three terminal areas (A, B and C). The main **tourist office** (⏲8.30am-8.30pm) is on the ground floor of Terminal 2B. Others on the ground floor of Terminal 2A and in Terminal 1 operate the same hours.

➡ **A1 Aerobús** (one-way/return €5.90/10.20; ⏲6am-1am) runs from the airport to Plaça de Catalunya (30 to 40 minutes) via Plaça d'Espanya and Gran Via de les Corts Catalanes every five to 10 minutes. Buy tickets on the bus or from machines at the airport.

➡ **R2 Nord train** (one-way €4.10; ⏲5.42am-11.38pm) leaves every half-hour from the airport via several stops to Estació de Sants (main train station, 20 minutes) and Passeig de Gràcia (25 to 30 minutes) in central Barcelona. The airport railway station is about a five-minute walk from Terminal 2.

➡ A taxi to the centre (around 30 minutes, depending on traffic) costs €25 to €30.

Aeroport de Girona–Costa Brava

Girona–Costa Brava Airport (☎902 404704; www.aena.es) is 12km south of Girona and 92km northeast of Barcelona. You'll find a tourist office, ATMs and lost-luggage desks on the ground floor.

➡ **Sagalés** (☎902 130014; www.sagales.com) runs the **Barcelona Bus** (☎902 130014; www.barcelonabus.com) service between Girona airport and Estació del Nord bus station in Barcelona (one way/return €14/21, 70 minutes).

Reus Airport

Reus Airport (☎902 404704; www.aena.es) is 13km west of Tarragona and 108km southwest of Barcelona. The tourist

---

Transport Tickets & Passes

➡ *Targetes* are multiple-trip tickets, sold at most Metro stations, that will save you time and money. A T-10 ticket (€10.30) gives you 10 trips on the Metro, buses and FGC trains; a T-DIA (€7.60) gives unlimited travel on all transport for one day.

➡ Hola BCN! two-/three-/four-/five-day tickets for unlimited travel on all transport excluding Aerobús cost €14/20/25.50/30.50.

---

office and lost luggage desks are in the main terminal building.

➡ **Hispano-Igualadina** (☎902 292900; www.igualadina.net; Estació Sants) bus services run between Reus airport and Estació d'Autobusos de Sants to meet flights (90 minutes, one-way/return €15/26).

Getting Around

Bicycle

☑ **Best for...** Scenic seaside rides.

➡ Barcelona has over 180km of bike lanes.

➡ A waterfront path runs northeast from Barceloneta to Port Olímpic and onwards to Riu Besòs.

➡ There are numerous places to hire bikes, particularly in Barri Gòtic and La Ribera. Note that the red 'Bicing' hire bikes are available for Barcelona residents only.

➡ You can transport your bicycle on the metro on weekdays (except between 7am and 9.30am, and 5pm and 8.30pm). On weekends, holidays, and during July and August, there are no restrictions.

Bus

☑ **Best for...** Night trips.

➡ **TMB buses** (☎010; www.tmb.net) run from 5am or 6am to as late as 11pm, depending on the line. Many routes pass through Plaça de Catalunya and/or Plaça de la Universitat.

➡ After 11pm a reduced network of yellow *nitbusos* (night buses) runs until 3am or 5am. All *nitbus* routes pass through Plaça de Catalunya and most run every 30 to 45 minutes. Single tickets cost €2.15 and can be purchased on the bus.

FGC

☑ **Best for...** Trips from Plaça de Catalunya to scattered attractions such as Tibidabo, Sarrià and Pedralbes.

➡ The **FGC** (www.fgc.net) suburban rail network goes numerous places that the Metro doesn't. It operates on a similar schedule and a one-way ticket costs €2.15.

Funicular

☑ **Best for...** Getting to and around Montjuïc.

➡ Cable cars connect La Barceloneta and Poble Sec with Montjuïc.

➡ The **Transbordador Aeri** (☎93 441 48 20; one-way/return/child under 7 €10/15/free; ⏱11am-8pm) service

runs from the Torre de Sant Sebastià (La Barceloneta) to Miramar (Montjuïc).

➡ The funicular railway runs from the Paral·lel Metro stop to the Estació Parc Montjuïc and is part of the Metro ticketing system.

➡ The **Telefèric de Montjuïc** (return €10.80; ⏱10am-9pm) runs from the Estació Parc Montjuïc to the Castell de Montjuïc at the summit of Montjuïc.

Metro

☑ **Best for...** Barcelona's Metro is almost always the best choice, with the most extensive network of lines and stations throughout the city. Exceptions include travel to Montjuïc and Sarrià.

➡ **Transports Metropolitans de Barcelona** (TMB; ☎010; www.tmb.net) runs the Metro system with eight colour-coded lines.

➡ Single tickets, good for one journey no matter how many changes you have to make, cost €2.15 and can be bought at Metro stations.

➡ The Metro operates from 5am to midnight

Sunday to Thursday, from 5am to 2am on Friday, and all night Saturday.

Taxi

☑ **Best for...** Quick trips across town outside peak hour.

➡ Taxis are reasonably priced and charges are posted on passenger-side windows inside. The trip from Plaça de Catalunya to Park Güell costs about €11.

➡ You can call a taxi or flag one down in the street. The leading operators are **Radio Taxi BCN** (☎93 225 00 00; www.radiotaxibcn.org), **Fonotaxi** (☎93 300 11 00) and **Radio Taxi Barcelona** (☎902 222111, 93 293 31 11).

Essential Information

Business Hours

☑ **Top Tip** Smaller shops in Barcelona close for an extended siesta, typically between 2pm and 4.30pm or 5pm.

Any exceptions to the following standard hours are noted in reviews:

Banks 8.30am-2pm Mon-Fri; some also 4-7pm Thu and 9am-1pm Sat

Central Post Offices 8.30am-9.30pm Mon-Fri, 8.30am-2pm Sat

Restaurants lunch 1-4pm, dinner 8pm-midnight

Shops 10am-2pm & 4.30-7.30pm or 5-8pm

Discount Cards

☑ **Top Tip** A great deal for culture lovers, **ArticketBCN** gives admission to six museums for €30. For more details, see the boxed text, p50.

The following cards (except student cards) are available at tourist offices:

ArqueoTicket (per person €13) Entry to five museums (Museu Marítim, Museu d'Història de Barcelona, Museu d'Arqueologia de Catalunya, Museu Egipci and Museu Barbier-Mueller d'Art Pre-Colombí).

Barcelona Card (www. barcelonacard.com; 2/3/4/5 days €34/44/52/58) Free

transport (and 20% off the Aerobús) and discounted admission (up to 30% off) or free entry to many sights. Cheaper if you book online, and kids' versions are available.

Ruta del Modernisme Discounts at Barcelona's main Modernista sights.

Student Cards Discounts of up to 50% at many sights.

Electricity

220V/230V/50Hz

Emergency

Ambulance ☑061

EU Standard Emergency Number ☑112

Fire ☑080 or ☑085

Police (Mossos d'Esquadra) ☑088

Money

The Spanish currency is the euro (€), divided into 100 cents.

ATMs Widely available; there is usually a charge on ATM cash withdrawals abroad.

Cash Banks and building societies offer the best rates; take your passport for ID.

Credit & Debit Cards Accepted in most hotels, restaurants and shops. May need to show passport or an alternative photo ID.

Money-Saving Tips

➡ Look out for free entry at sights.

➡ Order the *menú del día* for lunch in restaurants.

➡ Buy discount cards.

➡ Buy 10-trip travel cards to get around the city.

Public Holidays

Many shops will be closed and many attractions operate on reduced hours on the following dates:

New Year's Day 1 January

Epiphany 6 January

Good Friday Late March/April

Easter Monday Late March/April

Labour Day 1 May

Dilluns de Pasqua Grande (day after Pentecost Sunday) May/June

Feast of St John the Baptist 24 June

Feast of the Assumption 15 August

Catalonia's National Day 11 September

Festes de la Mercè 24 September

Spain's National Day 12 October

All Saints' Day 1 November

Constitution Day 6 December

Feast of the Immaculate Conception 8 December

Christmas Day 25 December

St Stephen's Day (Boxing Day) 26 December

Safe Travel

➡ Petty crime and theft, with tourists the prey of choice, is a problem in Barcelona, although most visitors encounter few problems. Take particular care on airport trains, the Metro (especially around stops popular with tourists) and La Rambla.

Telephone

Mobile Phones

➡ Local SIM cards are widely available and can be used in European and Australian mobile phones.

➡ US travellers will need to set their phones to roaming, or buy a local mobile and SIM card.

Phone Codes

Country code ☎34

International access code ☎00

Useful Numbers

International directory enquiries ☎11825

International operator & reverse charges Europe ☎1008, outside Europe ☎1005

Dos & Don'ts

Eating & drinking Waiters won't expect you to thank them every time they bring you something, but they will expect you to keep your cutlery between courses in more casual restaurants and bars.

Escalators Always stand on the right to let people pass, especially when using the metro.

Greetings Catalans, like other Spaniards, usually greet friends and strangers alike with a kiss on both cheeks, although two males rarely do this. Foreigners may be excused.

Visiting churches It is considered disrespectful to visit churches as a tourist during Mass and other worship services. Taking photos at such times is a definite no-no.

Toilets

➡ There are few public toilets in Barcelona, and cafes and bars are your best bet when in need. Make sure your chosen bar actually has a toilet before committing yourself.

Tourist Information

The **Oficina d'Informació de Turisme de Barcelona** (www.barcelonaturisme. com) has offices around the city:

Main Office (☎93 285 38 34; Plaça de Catalunya 17-S, underground; ☺9.30am-9.30pm; Ⓜ Catalunya)

Aeroport del Prat (Terminals 1 & 2 arrivals halls; ☺8.30am-8.30pm)

Barri Gòtic (Carrer de la Ciutat 2; ☺8.30am-8.30pm

Mon-Fri, 9am-7pm Sat, 9am-2pm Sun; Ⓜ Jaume I)

Estació de Sants (☺8am-8pm; Ⓜ Sants Estació)

Travellers with Disabilities

➡ Some hotels and many public institutions have wheelchair access.

➡ All buses and a growing number of metro stations are wheelchair accessible.

➡ Metro lines 2, 9, 10 and 11 are completely adapted, as are the majority of stops on Line 1.

➡ Ticket vending machines in metro stations are adapted for the disabled and have Braille options for the blind.

Accessible Barcelona (www.accessiblebarcelona. com) Craig Grimes, a T6

paraplegic and traveller, created this Barcelona-specific site; it's easily the most useful doorway into the city for travellers with disabilities.

Taxi Amic (☎93 420 80 88; www.terra.es/personal/taxiamic) A specialised taxi service for those with disabilities.

Visas

EU & Schengen Countries No visa required.

Australia, Canada, Israel, Japan, New Zealand and the USA No visa required for tourist visits of up to 90 days.

Other Countries Check with a Spanish embassy or consulate.

Language

Both Catalan (*català*) and Spanish (more precisely known as *castellano*, or Castilian) have official language status in Catalonia. In Barcelona you'll hear as much Spanish as Catalan and you'll find that most locals will happily speak Spanish to you, especially once they realise you're a foreigner. In this chapter, we've provided you with some Spanish to get you started, as well as some Catalan basics at the end.

Just read our pronunciation guides as if they were English and you'll be understood. Note that (m/f) indicates masculine and feminine forms.

To enhance your trip with a phrasebook, visit **lonelyplanet.com**. Lonely Planet iPhone phrasebooks are available through the Apple App store.

Basics

Hello.
Hola. — o·la

Goodbye.
Adiós. — a·dyos

How are you?
¿Qué tal? — ke tal

Fine, thanks.
Bien, gracias. — byen gra·thyas

Please.
Por favor. — por fa·vor

Thank you.
Gracias. — gra·thyas

Excuse me.
Perdón. — per·don

Sorry.
Lo siento. — lo syen·to

Yes./No.
Sí./No. — see/no

Do you speak (English)?
¿Habla (inglés)? — a·bla (een·gles)

I (don't) understand.
Yo (no) entiendo. — yo (no) en·tyen·do

Eating & Drinking

I'm a vegetarian. (m/f)
Soy vegetariano/a. — soy ve·khe·ta·rya·no/a

Cheers!
¡Salud! — sa·loo

That was delicious!
¡Estaba buenísimo! — es·ta·ba bwe·nee·see·mo

Please bring the bill.
Por favor nos trae la cuenta. — por fa·vor nos tra·e la kwen·ta

I'd like ...
Quisiera ... — kee·sye·ra ...

a coffee	*un café*	oon ka·fe
a table for two	*una mesa para dos*	oo·na me·sa pa·ra dos
a wine	*un vino*	oon vee·no
two beers	*dos cervezas*	dos ther·ve·thas

Shopping

I'd like to buy ...
Quisiera comprar ... — kee·sye·ra kom·prar ...

May I look at it?
¿Puedo verlo? — pwe·do ver·lo

How much is it?
¿Cuánto cuesta? — kwan·to kwes·ta

That's too/very expensive.
Es muy caro. — es mooy ka·ro

Can you lower the price?
¿Podría bajar un poco el precio? — po·dree·a ba·khar oon po·ko el pre·thyo

Emergencies

Help!
¡Socorro! so·ko·ro

Call a doctor!
¡Llame a lya·me a oon
un médico! me·dee·ko

Call the police!
¡Llame a lya·me a
la policía! la po·lee·thee·a

I'm lost. (m/f)
Estoy perdido/a. es·toy per·dee·do/a

I'm ill. (m/f)
Estoy enfermo/a. es·toy en·fer·mo/a

Where are the toilets?
¿Dónde están don·de es·tan
los baños? los ba·nyos

Time & Numbers

What time is it?
¿Qué hora es? ke o·ra es

It's (10) o'clock.
Son (las diez). son (las dyeth)

morning	*mañana*	ma·nya·na
afternoon	*tarde*	tar·de
evening	*noche*	no·che
yesterday	*ayer*	a·yer
today	*hoy*	oy
tomorrow	*mañana*	ma·nya·na

1	*uno*	oo·no
2	*dos*	dos
3	*tres*	tres
4	*cuatro*	kwa·tro
5	*cinco*	theen·ko
6	*seis*	seys
7	*siete*	sye·te
8	*ocho*	o·cho
9	*nueve*	nwe·ve
10	*diez*	dyeth

Transport & Directions

Where's ...?
¿Dónde está ...? don·de es·ta ...

What's the address?
¿Cuál es la kwal es la
dirección? dee·rek·thyon

Can you show me (on the map)?
¿Me lo puede me lo pwe·de
indicar een·dee·kar
(en el mapa)? (en el ma·pa)

I want to go to ...
Quisiera ir a ... kee·sye·ra eer a ...

What time does it arrive/leave?
¿A qué hora a ke o·ra
llega/sale? lye·ga/sa·le

I want to get off here.
Quiero bajarme kye·ro ba·khar·me
aquí. a·kee

Catalan – Basics

Good morning.
Bon dia. bon dee·a

Good afternoon.
Bona tarda. bo·na tar·da

Good evening.
Bon vespre. bon bes·pra

Goodbye.
Adéu. a·the·oo

Please.
Sisplau. sees·pla·oo

Thank you.
Gràcies. gra·see·a

You're welcome.
De res. de res

Excuse me.
Perdoni. par·tho·nee

I'm sorry.
Ho sento. oo sen·to

How are you?
Com estàs? kom as·tas

Very well.
(Molt) Bé. (mol) be

Behind the Scenes

Send Us Your Feedback

We love to hear from travellers – your comments help make our books better. We read every word, and we guarantee that your feedback goes straight to the authors. Visit **lonelyplanet.com/contact** to submit your updates and suggestions.

Note: We may edit, reproduce and incorporate your comments in Lonely Planet products such as guidebooks, websites and digital products, so let us know if you don't want your comments reproduced or your name acknowledged. For a copy of our privacy policy visit lonelyplanet.com/privacy.

Our Readers

Many thanks to the travellers who used the last edition and wrote to us with helpful hints, useful advice and interesting anecdotes: Caroline Amukusana, Chris Watts, Clara Winardi, Clive Ireland, Colin Charman, Emanuele Roserba, Tom Drinkwater

Manel Casanovas for gourmet insight at Barcelona Turisme, Sol Polo and friends, Margherita Bergamo, Carine Ferry, Gonzalo Salaya, Anna Aurich, Núria Rocamora, Manel Baena, Malén Gual and Bernardo Laniado-Romero. Thanks also to Alan Waterman for making the trip down from London. Finally, big hugs to my family for all their support.

Regis' Thanks

I'm grateful to the many friends and acquaintances who provided guidance and tips along the way. Biggest thanks go to Sal Davies for her hard work,

Acknowledgments

Cover photograph: La Sagrada Família, Neville Mountford-Hoare/4Corners.

This Book

This 4th edition of Lonely Planet's *Pocket Barcelona* guidebook was researched and written by Regis St Louis. The previous two editions were written by Anthony Ham and Damien Simonis. This guidebook was commissioned in Lonely Planet's London office, and produced by the following: **Coordinating Editor** Saralinda Turner **Product Editor** Kate Mathews **Destination Editor** Jo Cooke **Senior Cartographer** David Kemp **Book Designer** Katherine Marsh **Senior Editor** Karyn Noble **Assisting Editors** Bruce Evans, Tracy Whitmey **Cover Researcher** Naomi Parker **Thanks to** Elin Berglund, Ryan Evans, Larissa Frost, Jouve India, Indra Kilfoyle, Katie O'Connell, Martine Power, Eleanor Simpson, John Taufa, Dora Whitaker, Juan Winata

Index

See also separate subindexes for:

⊗ **Eating** p190

◯ **Drinking** p190

✿ **Entertainment** p191

🔒 **Shopping** p191

A

accommodation 176-8
activities 160, see also cycling, running, sports, surfing, swimming
airports 178-9
Ajuntament (Town Hall) 31
ambulance services 181
Antic Hospital de la Santa Creu 52
aquariums 80
architecture 154-5, see also Gaudí, Antoni
Berenguer i Mestres, Francesc 111
Cadafalch, Josep Puig i 96, 98, 100
contemporary 43, 154-5
Gaudí, Antoni 30, 100, 109
Gothic 68, 154-5
Miralles, Enric 66
Modernista 100, 144-5, 154-5
Montaner, Domènech i 96, 97
Montaner, Lluís Domènech i 109
Nouvel, Jean 130, 155

Sights 000
Map Pages 000

Roman 36
walking tour 144-5
area codes 182
art 128, 156-7, see also public artworks
Botero, Fernando 47
Casas, Ramon 104, 119
contemporary 43, 49, 56-9, 120-1, 128, 156
Dalí, Salvador 119, 128
El Greco 117
Fortuny, Mariano 119
Fra Angelico 117
Gehry, Frank 77
González, Julio 119
Gothic 117
Horn, Rebecca 80
Mir, Joaquim 119
Miró, Joan 11, 26, 120-1, 128, 157
Munch, Edvard 119
Picasso, Pablo 10, 56-9, 119, 128, 156
Ribera, Josep de 117
Romanesque 117
Sorolla, Joaquín 119
Tàpies, Antoni 96, 156
tickets 50
Zurbarán, Francisco de 117
ATMs 181

B

babysitting 164
Barceloneta, La 74-85, **76, 78-9**
drinking 84-5
food 82-4
itineraries 75, 76-7
shopping 85
sights 80-1
transport 75
Barri Gòtic 22-41, **30, 33-4**
drinking 38-40
entertainment 40-1
food 35-8
itineraries 23, 30-1, 142-3
shopping 41
sights 34-5
transport 23
bars 168-9, see also individual neighbourhoods, Drinking subindex
Basílica de Santa Maria del Mar 10, 60-1
bathrooms 183
beaches 158-9
bicycle travel, see cycling
Born Centre Cultural 66
budget 16, 181
bus travel 179-80
business hours 180

C

cable cars 180
cafes 170-1, see also individual neighbourhoods, Drinking subindex
CaixaForum 126
Camp Nou 11, 134-5
Casa Amatller 96
Casa Batlló 10, 90-1
Casa de les Punxes 98
Casa Lleó Morera 96
Casa-Museu Gaudí 113
Castell de Montjuïc 126
Catalan culture 23, 31
Catalan history 83
Catalan language 185
cell phones 16, 182
Centre d'Art Santa Mònica 27
Centre de Cultura Contemporània de Barcelona 50
children, travel with 164-5
chiringuitos 85
chocolate 171
climate 176
clubs 172, see also Drinking and Entertainment subindexes
Coin & Stamp Market 31
Columbus, Christopher 27

CosmoCaixa 163
costs 16, 181
credit cards 181
currency 16
cycling 84, 160, 179

D
Dalí, Salvador 119, 128
dance 31
debit cards 181
disabilities, travellers with 183
discount cards 50, 181
drinking 168-9, see also individual neighbourhoods, Drinking subindex

E
El Raval 42-53, **46, 48**
drinking 51-3
food 50-1
itineraries 43, 46-7, 142-3
shopping 53
sights 44-5, 49-50
transport 43
electricity 16, 181
Els Encants Vells 151
emergencies 181
entertainment, see also individual neighbourhoods, Entertainment subindex
Església de Betlem 25
Església de Sant Pau del Camp 50
Església de Santa Maria del Pi 34

Sights 000
Map Pages **000**

Església de Sants Just i Pastor 30
etiquette 182

F
farmers market 31
FC Barcelona 11, 134-5, 160
FGC trains 17, 180
fire services 181
Font Màgica 129
food 38, 146-7, 148-9, 152-3, see also individual neighbourhoods, Eating subindex
football 11, 134-5, 160
free attractions 167
Fundació Antoni Tàpies 96
Fundació Fran Daurel 126
Fundació Joan Miró 11, 120-1
Fundació Suñol 98
Fundación Francisco Godia 97
funicular railways 17, 180

G
galleries 156-7
gardens 158-9
Gaudí, Antoni 30, 100, 109, 155
Casa Batlló 10, 90-1
Casa Calvet 101
Jardins del Palau de Pedralbes 137
La Catedral
La Pedrera 11, 88-9
La Sagrada Família 8, 106-9
Palau Güell 49
Park Güell 9, 112-13
Plaça Reial 27

gay travellers 173
Gothic architecture 68, 154-5
Gothic art 117
Gràcia 110-11, **110**
Gran Teatre del Liceu 26-7

H
highlights 8-11, 12-13
history 37, 83
holidays 182
Hospital de la Santa Creu i Sant Pau 109

I
immigration 16, 183
internet resources 16, 176-7
itineraries 14-15, 142-7, see also individual neighbourhoods

J
Jardí Botànic 129
Jardins del Mirador 127
Jardins del Palaude Pedralbes 137
Jardins de Mossèn Cinto de Verdaguer 129

L
La Catedral 9, 28-9
La Pedrera 11, 88-9
La Rambla 9, 22-7, 26
La Rambla del Mar 80
La Ribera 54-73, **62, 64-5**
drinking 71
entertainment 71
food 69-70
itineraries 55, 62, 142-3

shopping 72-3
sights 56-61, 66-9
transport 55
La Sagrada Família 8, 106-9
L'Anella Olímpica & Estadi Olímpic 126-7
language 184-5
L'Aquàrium 80
L'Eixample 86-105, **92, 94-5**
drinking 103-4
food 98-103
itineraries 87, 92-3, 144-5
shopping 104-5
sights 88-91, 96-8
transport 87
lesbian travellers 173
live music 172, 174, see also Entertainment subindex

M
MACBA 49
markets
Coin & Stamp Market 31
Els Encants Vells 151
farmers market 31
Mercat de la Barceloneta 77
Mercat de la Boqueria 44-5
Mercat de la Llibertat 111
Mercat de Santa Caterina 66
Port Antic Market 82
menú del día 38
Mercat de la Barceloneta 77
Mercat de la Boqueria 10, 26, 44-5

Mercat de la Llibertat 111

Mercat de Santa Caterina 66

metro travel 180

Mirador de Colom 27

Miró, Joan 11, 26, 120-1, 128, 157

mobile phones 16, 182

Modernista architecture 100, 144-5, 154-5, see also Gaudí, Antoni

money 16, 181

Montaner, Lluís Domènech i 100

Montjuïc 114-31, 124-5

drinking 131

food 130-1

itineraries 115

sights 116-21, 126-9

transport 115

Mosaïc de Miró 26

Mossèn Costa i Llobera 127-9

MUHBA Refugi 307 129

Museu d'Arqueologia de Catalunya 129

Museu de Cera 27

Museu de la Xocolata 67

Museu de l'Eròtica 26

Museu del Disseny de Barcelona 155

Museu del Modernisme Català 97-8

Museu d'Història de Barcelona 34

Museu d'Història de Catalunya 77, 80

Museu Etnològic 129

Museu Europeu d'Art Modern 67-9

Museu Frederic Marès 34

Museu Marítim 81

Museu Nacional d'Art de Catalunya 11, 116-19

Museu Olímpic i de l'Esport 127

Museu Picasso 10, 56-9

Museu-Monestir de Pedralbes 137

museums 162-3

music 174

N

nightclubs 172, see also Drinking and Entertainment subindexes

O

Olympic sites 77, 126-7, 127

opening hours 180

P

Palau de la Generalitat 31

Palau de la Música Catalana 66

Palau de la Virreina 25

Palau del Baró Quadras 98

Palau Güell 49

Palau Montaner 96-7

Parc de Joan Miró 157

Parc de la Ciutadella 66

Park Güell 9, 112-13

parks 158-9

Parlament de Catalunya 66-7

Passeig de Gràcia 86-105, 92, 94-5

drinking 103-4

food 99-103

itineraries 87, 92-3

shopping 104-5

sights 88-91, 96-8

transport 87

Passeig de Joan de Borbó 77

Passeig del Born 62

Pedralbes 132-9, 136

drinking 139

entertainment 139

food 138-9

itineraries 133

sights 137

transport 133

Picasso, Pablo 10, 56-9, 119, 128, 156

Plaça de la Virreina 111

Plaça de Sant Josep Oriol 31, 143

Plaça de Vinçenç Martorell 46

Plaça Reial 27, 34

planning

budgeting 16, 181

children, travel with 164-5

itineraries 14-15

weather 176

websites 16, 176-7

Platja de la Barceloneta 77

Platja de Nova Icària 77

Platja de Sant Sebastià 77

Poble Espanyol 126

Poble Sec 114-31, 122, 124-5

drinking 131

entertainment 131

food 130-1

itineraries 115, 122-3

sights 126-9

transport 115

police 181

Port Antic Market 82

Port Olímpic 77

public artworks

Dona i Ocell 157

Gat 47

Homenatge a la Barceloneta 80

Mosaïc de Miró 26

Peix (Fish) 77

public holidays 182

R

Rambla del Raval 47

restaurants 148, see also individual neighbourhoods, Eating subindex

Roman ruins 35, 36

running 160

S

safety 182

Sant Antoni 114-31, 122, 124-5

drinking 131

food 130-1

itineraries 115, 122-3

sights 126-9

transport 115

sardana 31

Sarrià 132-9, 136

food 138-9

itineraries 133, 138

sights 137

transport 133

shopping 150-1, see also individual neighbourhoods, Shopping subindex

Sinagoga Major 34-5

soccer 11, 134-5, 160

spas 160

Aire De Barcelona 70

sports 160

surfing 81, 160

swimming 81, 160

T

tapas 152-3
Tàpies, Antoni 96, 156
taxis 180
telephone services
16, 182
**Temple Romà
d'August 35**
time 16
tipping 16
toilets 183
tourist information 183
tours 166, *see also* walks
train travel 180
Transbordador Aeri 80
transport 17, 178-80

U

**Universitat de
Barcelona gardens
98**

V

vacations 182
views 161
visas 16, 183

W

walks 142-7, 166
weather 176
websites 16, 176-7

🍴 Eating

5º Pino 138

A

Alba Granados 102
Allium 38
Amaltea 102

Sights 000
Map Pages **000**

B

Baluard Barceloneta 77
Bangkok Cafe 139
Bar Pinotxo 51
Bar Tomàs 138-9
Barraca 82
Belmonte 36
Bodega 1900 122

C

Cafè de l'Acadèmia 35
Cafè del Centre 171
Cafè de l'Òpera 40
Čaj Chai 40
Cal Boter 111
Cal Pep 69
Can Culleretes 31
Can Majó 82
Can Maño 82
Can Recasens 149
Caravelle 50-1
Casa Calvet 101
Casa Delfín 63
Cata 1.81 99
Cerveseria Catalana
101
Cinc Sentits 98-9
Comerç 24 69-70
Cosmo 93
Cova Fumada 77
Cremeria Toscana 102-3
Cuines de Santa
Caterin 70

E

El Atril 69
El Ben Plantat 84
El Cangrejo Loco 84
El Quim 45
Elisabets 47
Els Quatre Gats 38
En Aparté 70

F

Fàbrica Moritz 130
Fastvínic 102
Federal 123
Foix de Sarrià 139

G

Granja La Pallaresa 31
Granja M Viader 47

J

Jai-Ca 82
Joan La Llar del Pernil
45

K

Koy Shunka 36

L

La Bodegueta Provença
102
La Llavor dels Orí-
gens 70
La Nena 111
La Panxa del Bisbe 113
La Tomaquera 131
La Vinateria del
Call 36

M

Maians 82
Mam i Teca 50

P

Passadís del Pep 69
Pla 36

Q

Quimet i Quimet 130

R

Rasoterra 36-8

S

Salterio 40
Santana 138
Sésamo 51
Speakeasy 99
Suculent 51

T

Taktika Berri 99
Tapas 24 99
Taverna Can Margarit
130
Tickets 130

V

Vivanda 138

🍷 Drinking

A

Absenta 84
Antilla BCN 103
Astoria 104

B

Bar Calders 123
Bar del Pla 63
Bar Kasparo 46
Bar Leo 77
Bar Marsella 47
Bar Pastís 53
Bar Ramón 123
Barcelona Pipa Club 39
Boadas 51-2
Bormuth 63
Bubó 63

C

Can Paixano 76
Casa Almirall 52
CDLC 85

D

Dry Martini 103

E

El Xampanyet 63
Euskal Etxea 63

G

Gran Bodega Saltó 123

J

Juanra Falces 71

K

Ké? 84

L

La Caseta Del Migdia 131
La Confitería 52
La Fira 103
La Terrrazza 131
La Vinya del Senyor 71
Les Gens Que J'Aim 103
Lizarran 139

M

Manchester 40
Marmalade 52
Marula Cafè 40
Michael Collins Pub 107
Miramelindo 63
Moog 52-3
Mudanzas 71

O

Ocaña 38
Oviso 39

R

Raïm 111
Rouge Lab 2.1 123
Rubí 71

S

Santa Marta 85
Sor Rita 38-9

T

Tinta Roja 123

V

Vaso de Oro 77

🎭 Entertainment

Bikini 139
Filmoteca de Catalunya 51
Gran Teatre del Liceu 40
Harlem Jazz Club 40-1
Jamboree 41
Jazz Sí Club 47
Palau de la Música Catalana 71
Parc d'Atraccions 165
Sala Apolo 123
Teatre Mercat De Les Flors 131

🛍 Shopping

A

Adolfo Domínguez 105
Arlequí Màscares 72

B

Bagués-Masriera 93

C

Cacao Sampaka 93
Caelum 41
Camper 104-5
Casa Gispert 72
Coin & Stamp Market 31
Coquette 73
Custo Barcelona 72

D

Discos Castelló 47

E

El Bulevard dels Antiquaris 104
El Corte Inglés 104
El Magnífico 73
Els Encants Vells 151
Empremtes de Catalunya 41

F

Fantastik 53
Farmers' Market 31
Fires, Festes i Tradicions 41

H

Hofmann Pastisseria 72

J

Joan Múrria 104

L

La Manual Alpargatera 41
La Portorriqueña 53
Loewe 93
Loisaida 72
Lurdes Bergada 93

M

Maremàgnum 85
Mauri 93
Monvínic 93
Mushi Mushi 111

N

Nobodinoz 111
Nostàlgic 111

O

Olisoliva 73

P

Port Antic Market 82

R

Regia 105

V

Vila Viniteca 73
Vinçon 92

Our Writer

Regis St Louis

Regis first fell in love with Barcelona and Catalonia on a grand journey across Iberia in the late 1990s. Since then he has returned frequently, learning Spanish and a smattering of Catalan, and delving into the rich cultural history of this endlessly fascinating city. Favourite memories from his most recent trip include earning a few scars at a wild *correfoc* (fire-running) in Gràcia, watching brave *castellers* build human towers at the Santa Eulàlia fest and feasting on *navallas* (razor clams), *pop á feira* (Galician-style octopus) and *carxofes* (artichokes) all across town. Regis is also the author of *Discover Barcelona*, and he has contributed to *Spain*, *Portugal* and dozens of other Lonely Planet titles. He lives in Brooklyn, New York.

Published by Lonely Planet Publications Pty Ltd
ABN 36 005 607 983
4th edition – Nov 2014
ISBN 978 1 74220 891 6
© Lonely Planet 2014   Photographs © as indicated 2014
10 9 8 7 6 5 4 3 2 1
Printed in China